EGYPTIAN LEGENDS FOR KIDS

Mummies, Pharaohs, Queens, Gods & Myths from Ancient Egypt

History Brought Alive

© Copyright 2024 - All rights reserved.

The content contained within this book may not be reproduced, duplicated or transmitted without direct written permission from the author or the publisher.
Under no circumstances will any blame or legal responsibility be held against the publisher, or author, for any damages, reparation, or monetary loss due to the information contained within this book, either directly or indirectly.

Legal Notice:

This book is copyright protected. It is only for personal use. You cannot amend, distribute, sell, use, quote or paraphrase any part, or the content within this book, without the consent of the author or publisher.

Disclaimer Notice:

Please note the information contained within this document is for educational and entertainment purposes only. All effort has been executed to present accurate, up to date, reliable, complete information. No warranties of any kind are declared or implied. Readers acknowledge that the author is not engaged in the rendering of legal, financial, medical or professional advice. The content within this book has been derived from various sources.

Please consult a licensed professional before attempting any techniques outlined in this book.

By reading this document, the reader agrees that under no circumstances is the author responsible for any losses, direct or indirect, that are incurred as a result of the use of the information contained within this document, including, but not limited to, errors, omissions, or inaccuracies.

Contents

INTRODUCTION 1

CHAPTER 1: THE MIGHTY PHARAOHS 5

CHAPTER 2: QUEENS OF THE NILE 37

CHAPTER 3: THE MYSTERIOUS MUMMIES 62

CHAPTER 4: GODS AND GODDESSES 75

CHAPTER 5: MYTHS OF ANCIENT EGYPT 106

CHAPTER 6: HEROES AND LEGENDS 135

CONCLUSION 149

THE EXTRA PART 151
ANSWERS 154

THE EXTRA, EXTRA PART 155
ANSWERS 157

INTRODUCTION

Welcome, young adventurers, to the enchanting world of "Egyptian Legends for Kids!" Under the golden sands of the Nile River valley lie mysteries and wonders waiting to be discovered. Are you ready to embark on an unforgettable journey through time, where ancient pharaohs, mighty gods, and legendary heroes await?

In this captivating book, we will delve deep into the heart of ancient Egypt. This land is steeped in history, mythology, and intrigue. From the majestic pyramids of Giza to the mystical rituals of mummification, each chapter is filled with tales of valor, wisdom, and adventure that will spark your imagination and ignite your curiosity.

Chapter 1: The Mighty Pharaohs

Our journey begins with the mighty pharaohs. These characters were the revered rulers of ancient Egypt who wielded power and authority over the land. You will meet Tutankhamun, the boy king whose golden tomb held secrets beyond imagination. You will also discover Djoser, the visionary pharaoh who built the very first pyramid, and Ramses II, the great and powerful ruler whose reign stretched across the ages.

But our adventure doesn't stop there! You'll learn about Akhenaten, the heretic king who challenged tradition with his radical religious revolution, and Khufu, the builder of the Great Pyramid of Giza. Join us as we unravel the stories of these legendary figures and uncover the mysteries of their reigns.

Chapter 2: Queens of the Nile

In this chapter, we'll turn our gaze to the powerful queens who stood alongside the pharaohs. These women shaped the destiny of Egypt with their grace and strength. From Nefertiti, the beautiful queen who captured the hearts of her people, to Cleopatra, the last queen whose Roman ties changed the course of history, these remarkable women left a long-lasting mark on the sands of time.

Chapter 3: The Mysterious Mummies

Next, prepare to journey into the realm of the afterlife as we explore the ancient art of mummification. You'll learn about the intricate process of preserving a body for eternity and uncover the secrets hidden within the tombs of Egypt's illustrious pharaohs. From beliefs about the afterlife to the exploration of Egyptian graves, this chapter will unravel the mysteries of mummification and its significance in ancient Egyptian culture.

Chapter 4: Gods and Goddesses

After discovering the mysteries of the afterlife, you'll step into the realm of the gods and goddesses. These were the mighty deities who ruled over the heavens and the earth.

From Ra, the radiant sun god, to Osiris, the benevolent ruler of the dead, each deity holds a unique place in the pantheon of Egyptian mythology. Join us as we unravel the stories of these divine beings and explore the ancient mysteries of those who worshiped them.

Chapter 5: Myths of Ancient Egypt

When you've discovered the secrets of the gods and goddesses of ancient Egypt, you'll continue by embarking on a journey through the myths and legends of ancient Egypt. These stories describe heroic sailors who braved the seas, wise scribes who recorded their adventures, and ancient artifacts that revealed the secrets of the past. From the creation myth of Heliopolis to the legendary adventures of

Sphinx, each tale is a window into the rich tapestry of Egyptian folklore and tradition.

Chapter 6: Heroes and Legends

In our final chapter, we'll celebrate the heroes and legends that shaped the course of Egyptian history. Meet Imhotep, the architect who became a god, and Sinuhe, the adventurous scribe (someone who copied books and worked as a professional writer) whose tales captivate the imagination. Discover the wisdom of Ptah-hotep, the wise vizier (government official), and journey with Moses as he leads his people to freedom. From Ibn Khaldun, the great philosopher, to Muhammad Ali, the father of modern Egypt, these remarkable figures inspire us with their courage, wisdom, and resilience.

So, young adventurers, are you ready to embark on this extraordinary journey through the land of the pharaohs? Prepare to unlock the secrets of ancient Egypt! Let's embark on an adventure that will leave you spellbound and eager for more.

Now, let the magic of "Egyptian Legends for Kids" ignite your imagination and transport you to an ancient world of wonder!

CHAPTER 1: THE MIGHTY PHARAOHS

Welcome, dear readers, to the first chapter of our journey through the sands of ancient Egypt—a land where gods and mortals walked side by side and mighty pharaohs ruled with divine authority. In this chapter, we will dive into the world of the pharaohs. We will explore their roles, stories, and those legacies which have echoed through the corridors of time.

The pharaohs were more than just kings; in fact, they were respected as living gods that were entrusted with the sacred duty of maintaining order, harmony, and prosperity throughout their kingdom. Because they acted as a divine messenger between the mortal realm and the gods, pharaohs wielded unparalleled power and authority. They commanded loyalty and devotion from their subjects. Our journey begins with tales of some of the most renowned pharaohs of ancient Egypt, whose names have been whispered on desert winds throughout centuries of history.

Tutankhamun: The Boy King and His Golden Tomb

In the land of ancient Egypt, where the mighty Nile River flows and the pyramids touch the sky, there once lived a young king named Tutankhamun. Though his name might be a mouthful, you can simply call him King Tut. His story is one of mystery and treasure. It began over 3,000 years ago!

The Young King

King Tut became pharaoh when he was about nine years old—imagine being a king in third or fourth grade! He was so young that people often called him the "Boy King." During a time when Egypt was filled with splendid palaces and grand monuments, young Tutankhamun had a very big role. But what is really fascinating wasn't just his age; rather, it's the incredible story of how he was discovered many years later.

A Tomb Lost and Found

For thousands of years, the sands of Egypt hid King Tut's tomb from the world. It's true that many pharaohs had grand tombs filled with treasures, but over time, robbers had taken almost all of them.

King Tut's tomb, however, was different. It lay hidden under the sands, keeping its secrets and treasures safe, waiting to be discovered.

It wasn't until 1922 that a British explorer named Howard Carter found a step cut into the rock of the Valley of the Kings. After some careful digging, he uncovered a doorway, and behind it was the tomb of King Tut! Imagine finding a secret door that no one had opened for over 3,000 years!

Treasures Galore

When Howard Carter opened the tomb, he couldn't believe his eyes. There was treasure everywhere! He saw golden statues, jewelry, chariots, and even King Tut's throne. But the most amazing of the treasures was King Tut's coffin that was made of solid gold. Inside, the young king's mummy wore a magnificent golden mask that showed his youthful face, calm and serene.

Carter found rooms filled with things a king might need in the afterlife. There were clothes, weapons, and even toys from Tut's childhood—things he loved when he was probably about your age! Because Egyptians believed that life after death was very similar to life on earth, they buried their dead with everything they thought they might need.

The Curse of the Pharaohs

However, this wouldn't be a good treasure story without a bit of mystery. When Carter found King Tut's tomb, rumors started about a "curse" that would affect anyone who entered the tomb. Newspapers told spooky stories of bad luck and strange occurrences that happened to those who visited the tomb. But, don't worry, these stories are just myths. In fact, many people involved in the tomb's discovery lived long and happy lives.

Why King Tut is Famous

So, why is King Tut so famous if he was so young and did not stay pharaoh for very long? Well, it's because his tomb gives us a glittering window into Egypt's past. As previously mentioned, most royal tombs were emptied by robbers long ago. Tut's tomb, however, was full of treasures that help us understand how the ancient Egyptians lived, what they believed, and how they celebrated their kings.

King Tut teaches us that you don't have to be the biggest or the oldest to be remembered. Sometimes, being a part of a great discovery is enough to make you famous forever, like King Tut—the Boy King whose golden tomb helped us discover the wonders of ancient Egypt.

Djoser: The Visionary Pharaoh

After discovering the mysteries of the afterlife through King Tut, next we'll delve deep into the life and legacy of a pharaoh who ushered in an era of progress and innovation to ancient Egypt. This extraordinary ruler's name was Pharaoh Djoser.

Pharaoh Djoser's most enduring legacy is undoubtedly the magnificent Step Pyramid. This pyramid is located in the sprawling necropolis (or, a cemetery filled with elaborate tombs) of Saqqara. This awe-inspiring structure, which rises majestically from the desert sands, stands as a testament not only to Djoser's vision but also the ingenuity of ancient Egyptian craftsmanship. Built under the guidance of Djoser's brilliant architect, Imhotep, the Step Pyramid revolutionized funerary architecture and laid the foundation for future pyramid construction.

Economic Revitalization

Djoser's accomplishments, however, extended far beyond the realm of monumental construction. He was a forward-thinking ruler who recognized that economic development was vital to ensure the prosperity of his kingdom. Djosein began ambitious mining expeditions across Egypt to tap into the nation's rich natural resources. His copper mines yielded precious metal for tools and weapons, while turquoise mines provided gemstones for beautiful jewelry. Furthermore, Djoser understood trade dynamics, which enabled him to negotiate profitable deals with neighboring regions.

Agricultural Innovation

In addition to his efforts in mining and trade, Djoser implemented groundbreaking reforms in agriculture, which was essential to Egypt's prosperity. Djoser recognized that the Nile River was vital to the kingdom's agricultural success. So, he oversaw the construction of irrigation canals and reservoirs to ensure the water was distributed to farmland. These innovative irrigation systems transformed desert landscapes into fertile fields. These systems also enhanced crop yields and ensured food security for Egypt's growing population.

Legacy of Leadership

Pharaoh Djoser's reign was characterized by bold initiatives and forward-thinking policies that propelled Egypt to new heights of prosperity and influence. His unwavering commitment to innovation and progress left a permanent mark on the ancient world, which went on to inspire future generations of rulers and visionaries. Today, as we marvel at the incredible Step Pyramid and reflect on Djoser's enduring legacy, we are reminded of the importance of imaginative leadership and the potential of human achievements.

Ramses II: The Great and Powerful Ruler

After exploring the impressive innovations and architectural achievements of Djoser, we will visit one of the most remarkable kings of ancient Egypt,

Ramses the Great. This pharaoh was famous not just for his power in battle, but also for building some of the most awe-inspiring monuments that we can still see today!

Ramses II, or Ramses the Great, was a pharaoh of the Nineteenth Dynasty. He ruled Egypt for an impressive 66 years—from his teenage years all the way into his nineties! During his reign, Egypt enjoyed peace and prosperity. People were happy, crops grew well, and there was plenty of food for everyone. But Ramses, however, didn't just want to be remembered for that; he wanted to be remembered forever.

A King and His Monuments

So, Ramses began building incredible temples and statues to leave his mark on Egypt forever. If you've ever seen pictures of giant statues with faces that look like they're gazing down at you, you may have been looking at some of Ramses' work!

The Temple of Abu Simbel

One of his most famous projects is the Temple of Abu Simbel. This temple was carved out of a mountainside, and has four huge statues of Ramses himself. Each statue is about as tall as a house!

Inside the temple, the walls are decorated with carvings that tell the story of Ramses's victories in battle and blessings from the gods. Twice a year, the sun shines directly into the heart of this temple, lighting up the sculptures on the back wall. Only one statue remains unlit, which displays the god of the underworld. This magical event shows how knowledgeable the ancient Egyptians were in relation to astronomy and architecture.

The Ramesseum

Another amazing building project by Ramses is the Ramesseum, his funerary temple in the Valley of the Kings. This massive temple was not just a place for worship, but also a place to celebrate his reign and achievements. It once featured a gigantic statue of Ramses that weighed over 1,000 tons—that's as heavy as 200 elephants!

Ramses the War Hero

Ramses wasn't just good at building; he was also a brave warrior. One of his most famous battles was the Battle of Kadesh. Ramses led his army against the Hittites, a powerful group of people that wanted to take over Egyptian territories. The battle was fierce, and though both sides claimed victory, Ramses used this event to boost his image as a strong and invincible leader. At his command, the story of the battle was carved on temples all across Egypt so everyone knew about Ramses's bravery.

Why We Remember Ramses the Great

Today, we don't only remember Ramses because he was a powerful king. Ramses also left us with some of the most incredible Egyptian monuments that we can still visit today. These constructions tell us a lot about the ancient Egyptians—how they lived, what was important to them, and their worldview.

Ramses also made sure that his deeds and stories were carved on the walls of these temples. Because of this, we know about his battles, his family, and even his favorite hobbies! It's like he made a stone time capsule for us to discover thousands of years later.

Ramses the Great, his grand monuments, and thrilling battle stories, now teach us an important lesson: what we create and do in our lives can tell our story long after we're gone. Thanks to Ramses' efforts, we can still walk through the halls of his temples today and marvel at the same scenes he looked upon thousands of years ago. He made sure he would be remembered as more than a king of Egypt; rather, he made sure he was remembered as a legend.

Next time you build something—whether it's a sandcastle, a Lego tower, or a drawing—think about what story you want it to tell. Just like Ramses, you're creating something that tells your story!

Akhenaten: The Heretic King and his Religious Revolution

You'll soon learn that Ramses was not the only one who wanted to permanently shape Egyptian history. This pharaoh's name was Akhenaten, and he was one of the most unusual pharaohs in Egyptian history. Instead of worshiping lots of gods like everyone else, Akhenaten chose to worship just one god. Let's dive into the story of this bold king and his big changes!

Who Was Akhenaten?

Akhenaten was not always known by this name. When he became pharaoh, he was called Amenhotep IV. As time went on during his reign,

Akhenaten decided he was going to be different. About five years into his rule, Amenhotep changed his name to Akhenaten, which means "He who is of service to Aten." Aten was the sun disk, and according to Akhenaten, the only god that should be worshiped.

The City of the Sun

Akhenaten's first big move as pharaoh was to build a brand-new city in honor of his favorite god, Aten. He named this city Akhetaten, which means "Horizon of Aten." This city was located in the middle of Egypt, and it was where Akhenaten said Aten's (the sun's) rays were the strongest. Imagine a whole city built just to honor the sun!

In Akhetaten, big open-air temples were built so that everyone could feel the sun's rays. Akhenaten designed the temples this way because he believed that Aten's spirit was in the sunlight. So, unlike other dark, mysterious temples of Egypt, these were bright and filled with sunshine.

A New Art Style

Akhenaten also made another bold move by changing the way art was made in Egypt. Before Akhenaten, art in Egypt was formal and strict. Humans were usually shown in perfect, idealized forms. But Akhenaten liked art that was more relaxed and realistic. As such, art from his time shows him and his family in ways no one had ever seen pharaohs before—playing with their children, showing affection, and even looking less-than-perfect with long, exaggerated features.

Trouble with the Change

Not everyone liked these changes. Many people were upset because they loved their gods and did not want to worship only Aten. The priests who served other gods were especially unhappy because they lost a lot of power and money when people stopped worshiping their gods.

Because of all these changes, some people started calling Akhenaten the "Heretic King," which means he was someone who went against what everyone else believed. This was a big deal because, in ancient Egypt, keeping the gods happy was very important. People believed that if the gods were unhappy, bad things like famine or disease began.

After Akhenaten

Akhenaten ruled for about 17 years. After he died, things in Egypt quickly went back to the way they had been before. For example, the capital was moved back to the city of Thebes, and the temples of Aten were closed. The new pharaohs, including Tutankhamun (who was thought to be Akhenaten's son) decided it was better to go back to worshiping many gods instead of just one.

Why Akhenaten is Remembered

Even though his ideas didn't last, Akhenaten is one of the most famous pharaohs today because he dared to be different. His attempt to change the Egyptian religion was a big deal. His decision shows us that sometimes, being a leader means making hard decisions that not everyone will like.

Akhenaten's story helps us understand that history isn't just about what works; it's also about experiments and ideas that may not succeed but certainly make a mark. His city, art, and ideas tell us a lot about how one person tried to change the world around him. His story is about shining a light on new ideas, just like the sun's rays shining down on his city of Akhetaten.

Snefru: The Pyramid Builder

Long before the Great Pyramid of Giza stood tall, there was a pharaoh named Snefru. Snefru loved building pyramids so much that he built not one, not two, but three massive pyramids that transformed Egyptian architecture forever. Let's journey back to the time of Snefru, the king who set the stage for all pyramids that came after his.

Who Was Snefru?

Snefru was the first pharaoh of the Fourth Dynasty of Egypt, around 4,600 years ago. He is known as one of Egypt's most effective and ambitious builders. Unlike other pharaohs who were mostly remembered for their battles, Snefru was famous for his peaceful reign and his passion for giant building projects. In fact, he was so good at building that he is often called the "Pyramid King."

Snefru's Pyramid Adventures

The Meidum Pyramid

Snefru's first pyramid was actually at Meidum, which was originally a step pyramid built by his predecessor. Snefru converted it into a true pyramid by filling in the steps with limestone. However, this pyramid didn't turn out as well as he hoped—over time, it collapsed into a heap of rubble. But from this failure, Snefru learned many lessons about pyramid-building that he would use in his later constructions.

The Bent Pyramid

At Dahshur, you'll find Snefru's first big project called the Bent Pyramid. But, why is this pyramid bent? Well, it's because halfway through building it, the architects realized the angle was too steep, and the whole thing would collapse if they didn't make some quick changes. So, they changed the angle to make the pyramid rise more gently, which gave it a unique bent shape. They were practically learning how to build a pyramid while actually doing it!

The Red Pyramid

Not far from the Bent Pyramid, Snefru built another pyramid. This one was known as the Red Pyramid because of the reddish hue of its stones.

This pyramid was the first successful attempt at building a smooth-sided pyramid (which is what most of us think of when we imagine a pyramid). This great success made Snefru very proud, and it set the standard for all future pyramids in Egypt, including the most famous ones at Giza.

Snefru's Legacy

Snefru's pyramids were not just big piles of stones; they were marvels of engineering and symbols of divine kingship. They showed the power and glory of the pharaoh and ensured that Snefru would be remembered for millennia. Each pyramid was an improvement on the last, demonstrating Snefru's growing understanding of architecture and determination to perfect his craft.

Snefru's efforts paved the way for his son, Khufu, who would go on to build the Great Pyramid of Giza, which is one of the Seven Wonders of the Ancient World. Thanks to Snefru's innovations, Khufu had the knowledge and tools he needed to construct a pyramid that would stand as the tallest structure made by humans for thousands of years.

Why Snefru is a Hero

In the storybooks of Egyptian history, Snefru might not battle monsters or lead giant armies into war, but he still teaches us something very important:

that failure is just a step on the path to success. Though his first pyramid didn't quite work out, and his second one needed a big change halfway through, Snefru never gave up. He kept improving, and eventually, he achieved his dream of building Egypt's first smooth-sided pyramid.

So, remember Snefru not just for his pyramid building, but also for his problem solving and as a pioneer, who turned his dreams into reality through persistence and ingenuity. His story encourages us all to keep trying, learning, and building, no matter how challenging our goals may seem. Just like Snefru, you too can build something wonderful, one stone at a time!

Khufu: The Builder of the Great Pyramid

Our next ancient Egyptian king, Khufu (known to the Greeks as Cheops), was the second pharaoh of the Fourth Dynasty of ancient Egypt. He ruled over 4,500 years ago and is most famous for constructing the Great Pyramid of Giza. But Khufu was more than just a builder; he was also a powerful leader whose reign brought significant achievements in art and architecture.

The Great Pyramid of Giza

Imagine a structure so massive and that it was the tallest man-made structure in the world for nearly 4,000 years. This was the title that the Great Pyramid of Giza held until the Lincoln Cathedral was built in England in the 14th Century! This pyramid was originally built to be Khufu's tomb, meaning that it would've been a huge monument meant to display his power and ensure his journey to the afterlife. This pyramid is truly a marvel of engineering and architectural planning.

How Was It Built?

The Great Pyramid is made up of millions of limestone blocks, each weighing several tons. How the ancient Egyptians transported and assembled these blocks remains one of history's great mysteries. Some believe they used ramps, while others suggest a series of pulleys might have been involved. Despite modern technology and archaeological advances, the exact methods of construction still puzzle scientists and historians today.

Khufu believed that his great pyramid was not just his final resting place but also a staircase to heaven. This belief highlights the deep spiritual and religious significance of the pyramids, serving as a bridge between the earthly realm and the divine.

The Pyramid's Interior

Inside the Great Pyramid, the corridors and chambers are arranged with precision. The most famous room is the King's Chamber, which lies at the heart of the pyramid. Here, the walls are smooth, and the ceiling is made of large granite slabs. Those who have studied this pyramid believe these slabs relieved the weight from the layers of stone above them.

Visitors who tour the pyramid today will feel a direct connection to Egypt's distant past via the cool, narrow passages that lead to these ancient rooms.

Khufu's Legacy

Although not much is known about Khufu's reign beyond his pyramid, his legacy is monumental. His pyramid not only symbolizes the architectural achievements of ancient Egypt, but also how fascinating Egypt is in the collective imagination of people around the world.

Today, the Great Pyramid of Giza continues to be a symbol of Egypt's grandeur and has inspired countless tales, studies, and even replicas around the globe. It attracts millions of tourists each year, all eager to glimpse the majesty of the past.

Thutmose III: The Warrior Pharaoh

Though many ancient Egyptians are known for building the pyramids, other pharaohs are known for accomplishments in military strategy. Thutmose III was one of these successful pharaohs. He was part of the powerful Eighteenth Dynasty. He took the throne while he was still very young after the death of his stepmother, Hatshepsut, who had been his co-ruler for many years. So, once he became the sole ruler, Thutmose III proved himself as one of the most ambitious and successful military leaders in ancient history.

The Rise of a Warrior

Even as a young prince, Thutmose III showed great promise in military strategy and combat skills. When he took full control of the throne, Thutmose III wasted no time in expanding Egypt's empire. He led numerous military campaigns into lands such as Syria, Nubia, and the Near East, bringing these vast territories under Egyptian control.

One of Thutmose III's most famous military exploits was the Battle of Megiddo. This battle is considered one of the first to be well-documented in history, with detailed accounts recorded on the walls of the Temple of Karnak. Thutmose's army faced a large allied army of rebellious states led by the king of Kadesh. Instead of taking the easy routes to Megiddo, Thutmose chose a narrow pathway, surprising his enemies with his bold and risky move. His strategy was a success, and the victory at Megiddo was a turning point that solidified his reputation as a brilliant military leader.

The Empire Builder

Through his numerous campaigns, Thutmose III greatly expanded the borders of Egypt. He created an empire that stretched from northern Syria to deep into Nubia. His conquests also brought wealth and resources to Egypt, making it the most powerful and prosperous nation in the ancient world at that time. Thutmose III ensured that Egypt had control over crucial trade routes and demanded that his conquered lands supplied Egypt with gifts, which filled Egypt's coffers with gold, ivory, and precious woods.

Thutmose the Administrator

Thutmose III was not only a great warrior; he was also a skilled leader. He made sure that the empire he built was well-managed and organized. He appointed loyal officials to govern the new territories and established supply storerooms to support his army. He also built great temples and monuments to celebrate his victories and honor the gods, particularly Amun, whom he credited with his military success.

The Festival Temple of Thutmose III

Among his architectural achievements, the Festival Temple of Thutmose III at Karnak is especially notable. This temple was unique because it served as both a place of worship and a memorial of Thutmose's reign and military triumphs. The walls of the temple were decorated with inscriptions that detailed his military campaigns and celebrated his victories. This temple served as a historical record for future generations.

His Legacy

Thutmose III ruled Egypt for almost 54 years, during which he transformed the empire into an international superpower. His reign is often seen as a golden age of prosperity and power for ancient Egypt. After his death, he was worshiped as a god by the people he had ruled, a rare honor that only a few pharaohs received.

Thutmose III, the Warrior Pharaoh, was a ruler whose military genius and visionary leadership left a lasting mark on the world. His story teaches us about courage, strategy, and the importance of strong leadership. As we close this chapter on Thutmose III, remember that his battles and triumphs are not just ancient stories, but lessons on how determination and wisdom can lead to greatness.

Xerxes I: The Persian Pharaoh

Now we'll travel beyond the familiar borders of ancient Egypt to meet a ruler from a land far away—Xerxes I, also known as Xerxes the Great. He was not just any ruler; he was the "Achaemenid king" of Persia who also became known as a pharaoh of Egypt during the 27th Dynasty. Let's dive into the story of this intriguing figure!

Xerxes I ruled from 486 BC to 465 BC and was one of the most famous kings of the Achaemenid Empire. This empire was based in Persia, which is now modern-day Iran. His empire was huge, stretching from India to the edges of Greece. This included Egypt, which had been conquered by the Persians in 525 BC under his predecessor, Cambyses II.

Xerxes as Pharaoh

When Xerxes I took the throne, he inherited not just the Persian Empire but also its territories, including Egypt. As ruler of Egypt, he was recognized as a pharaoh, but his reign was markedly different from those of native Egyptian kings. Xerxes was seen by many Egyptians as an outsider, and his rule was characterized by a lack of respect for local Egyptian traditions.

A Tyrant in the Eyes of Many

Xerxes I's approach to governance caused the Egyptian people to dislike him. He was often described as a tyrant because he imposed Persian customs and ignored Egyptian religious and cultural practices. This disregard for local tradition made him unpopular, and many Egyptians longed for the return of a native ruler. The Greeks also did not like him. They thought he was a harsh ruler, especially because of his attempts to invade Greece.

The Invasion of Greece

One of Xerxes I's most ambitious military campaigns was when he attempted to conquer Greece. He mobilized a massive army and navy, and in 480 BC, he personally led these forces into Greece. There were many famous battles, such as those at Thermopylae and Salamis. Although initially successful, his campaign ultimately failed, and this defeat marked a turning point in his reign. It also cemented his reputation among the Greeks as a classic "bad guy" in their stories of heroism and resistance.

Despite his negative reputation, Xerxes I's rule had significant impacts on the regions he governed. In Egypt, his reign incorporated the Egyptian territory into the Persian Empire's administrative and economic systems. This period highlighted the complexities of empire-building and the challenges of managing diverse cultures within a single government.

Xerxes's Legacy

Xerxes's legacy is complicated. In Persia, he was remembered as a mighty king who tried to expand the boundaries of his empire, even if not always successfully. In Egypt, his legacy is more controversial because he didn't care about local customs and governance. His attempts to impose Persian authority on Egypt without embracing its rich cultural traditions left a lasting stain on the historical memory of his rule.

Xerxes I, the Persian Pharaoh, teaches us about the challenges and intricacies of ruling over a diverse empire. His story helps us understand that respect for local traditions and cultures is crucial in maintaining harmony within a society.

Chapter Conclusion

As we draw the curtain over the tales of these mighty pharaohs, we find ourselves immersed in the timeless beauty of ancient Egypt—a world where gods and mortals danced in the flickering light of eternity, and the echoes of greatness echoed through the ages.

From the golden treasures of Tutankhamun's tomb to the towering monuments of Ramses the Great, each pharaoh left their mark in the sands of time. But beyond the gold and granite lies a deeper truth—a testament to the resilience, intelligence, and boundless ambition of the human spirit. The pharaohs, with their towering monuments and divine authority, remind us of how humans share an enduring quest for immortality that transcends the boundaries of time.

As we bid farewell to the pharaohs and their timeless legacy, let us carry their stories in our hearts, like precious jewels gleaming in the darkness of the night. For in the heart of the desert, amidst the whispers of the gods, the spirit of the pharaohs lives on.

CHAPTER 2: QUEENS OF THE NILE

After taking a peek into the fascinating lives of the pharaohs, in this chapter, we will delve into the lives of the influential queens whose legacies burn brightly in Egyptian history. From the iconic beauty of Nefertiti to the mysterious reign of Queen Merneith, each queen's story offers a glimpse into the rich tapestry of Egyptian civilization. Their tales reveal the complexities of leadership, the pursuit of justice, and the enduring legacy of female empowerment in the ancient world.

Join us as we journey through the corridors of history to uncover the triumphs and challenges faced by these remarkable women who reigned as queens of the Nile. Prepare to be captivated by the tales of these extraordinary women who dared to defy convention and add their names into the sands of time.

Nefertiti: The Beautiful One Has Come

Long ago, in the sunny land of Egypt, there lived a queen so beautiful and wise that her story has been told for over 3,000 years. Her name was Nefertiti, which means "The Beautiful One Has Come," but she was also as clever as she was pretty. Let's dive into her powerful story!

Who Was Nefertiti?

Nefertiti was the wife of Pharaoh Akhenaten (remember this pharaoh who was obsessed with the sun god?), and together they ruled Egypt during a time of big changes. She is famous not just for her stunning beauty but also for her powerful role in Egypt's cultural and religious revolution. Nefertiti wasn't born a royal, but she became one of the most influential queens Egypt ever saw.

A Queen and Her King

Nefertiti and her husband, Akhenaten, did something extraordinary when they became the rulers of Egypt. As previously mentioned, they decided that instead of worshiping many gods, as people in Egypt had done for centuries, they would worship only one god, Aten, the sun disk. This was a huge change! Akhenaten and Nefertiti moved the capital to a new city called Akhetaten (now known as Amarna), dedicated to their new god.

Nefertiti didn't just sit around looking pretty; she shared power with Akhenaten. She took on roles that were usually reserved for kings. In artwork created in that time, Nefertiti is often shown driving a chariot or cutting down Egypt's enemies. This proved that Nefertiti was more than just a wife; she was a co-ruler.

The Famous Bust of Nefertiti

One of the reasons we remember Nefertiti so well is because of a stunning piece of art. During a German archaeologist's dig in 1912, a beautifully painted bust (a type of sculpture that displays the head and face of an important person) of Nefertiti was found. This bust, now in Berlin, shows her with a long, graceful neck, a perfectly symmetrical face, and a colorful crown. It's so lifelike that it almost seems like she could start talking at any moment!

Nefertiti's Mysterious End

Towards the end of Akhenaten's reign, Nefertiti disappears from historical records. So, what happened to her remains a mystery. Some believe she might have died, while others think she may have ruled Egypt on her own as the Pharaoh Neferneferuaten after her husband's death. This mystery makes her story even more fascinating.

Why Nefertiti is Important

Nefertiti is an icon of beauty and power. She shows us that ancient queens were not just royal wives but could also be influential leaders and reformers that ruled empires and made history. Her life tells a story of courage, change, and mystery that captures the imagination of people all around the world, even today.

The story of Nefertiti also teaches us about the importance of art, leadership, and innovation. She and her husband tried to change Egyptian society in ways that were far ahead of their time. Though not all these changes lasted, their attempt shows us that it's okay to think differently and try new things, even if they don't turn out as expected.

So, as you flip through the pages of history, remember Nefertiti, the beautiful queen who left a lasting mark. Her story isn't just about ancient Egypt; it's about the timeless beauty and strength that lives in all of us, waiting to be discovered.

Queen Merneith: The Mysterious Ruler of the Nile

Meet one of the most puzzling figures of ancient Egypt—Queen Merneith. Her story takes us all the way back to Egypt's First Dynasty, around 2920 BCE. Let's uncover the secrets of this possibly first female ruler of Egypt, whose life is shrouded in mystery.

Queen Merneith may have been one of the earliest women to rule ancient Egypt, but much about her life remains a puzzle. Unlike famous pharaohs whose stories fill the pages of history books, Merneith's tale is pieced together from small clues left behind over millennia. She lived so long ago that only a few records of her name survive, mainly on some artifacts and a tomb that might be hers.

A Queen or a Regent?

Historians are not entirely sure if Queen Merneith was a pharaoh or a regent, which means she might have ruled on behalf of her young son, Den, who was too young to govern. This situation wasn't uncommon in ancient times—often, when a king died and his heir was too young, a trusted family member, usually the mother, would rule until the child was old enough.

Her Powerful Role

What we know about Merneith suggests that she was a woman of significant power and status. She is listed among the kings of the First Dynasty in a document from much later times, which hints that she was not just a caretaker but a ruler. Her burial site also supports this idea. Merneith was buried in a large and richly furnished tomb at Abydos, one of ancient Egypt's most sacred burial grounds. Her tomb was surrounded by those of other pharaohs, a place of honor that suggests she was much more than just a royal family member.

Queen Merneith's tomb is especially remarkable because it shows how respected she was. Archaeologists found that she was buried alongside 50 servants, who were laid to rest with her to serve her in the afterlife. This was a royal privilege, underscoring her high rank and the respect she commanded within the kingdom.

Because there are so few records, much about Queen Merneith's reign is left to our imagination. Did she lead battles? Did she oversee the construction of monuments? Did she make laws? These are questions that might never be answered.

However, the fact that she was buried among kings tells us that her people valued her leadership and likely saw her as a capable and strong ruler.

Why Her Story Matters

Queen Merneith's story is important because it shows us that women in ancient Egypt could rise to the highest levels of power. Her legacy helps us understand the role of women in ancient Egyptian society, where people could respect and honor a woman as a leader. Her story also excites historians and archaeologists who continue to search for clues about her life and reign.

So, dear friends, as we close this chapter on Queen Merneith, remember that history is often like a puzzle. With every small piece we find, we get a clearer picture of the past. Queen Merneith reminds us that even those from long ago, whose names are barely remembered, can still have stories worth telling.

Hatshepsut: The Queen Who Became King

Unlike Merneith, other ancient Egyptian women are more understood via artifacts and other records. Hatshepsut was one of these women. She was a princess that was born into a family of pharaohs. Her father was Thutmose I, so she grew up surrounded by the riches and power of the Egyptian court. But Hatshepsut was no ordinary princess; she had great ambition and intelligence that set her apart from others.

After her father's death, Hatshepsut didn't follow the typical path expected for women at the time. Instead, she became Egypt's queen by marrying her half-brother Thutmose II (this was a custom for royals). But when he died young, Hatshepsut did something extraordinary—she declared herself pharaoh instead of a queen. She even began to dress like a king and wear a false beard, symbols of pharaonic power. This was nearly unheard of in the male-dominated world of ancient Egyptian royalty!

Her Reign as Pharaoh

As pharaoh, Hatshepsut was not just playing dress-up; she was a powerful and effective leader. She ruled for about 22 years and brought great prosperity to Egypt. Her reign was a time of peace and economic flourishing. She increased trade with distant lands and built magnificent temples that still stand today as a testament to her reign.

The Expedition to Punt

One of Hatshepsut's most famous achievements was her trading expedition to the mysterious land of Punt, which is thought to have been near the Red

Sea or along the coasts of East Africa. This expedition brought back loads of treasures, such as gold, exotic spices, and ivory. Live myrrh trees were also brought back and planted in the temple gardens. The success of this voyage was celebrated in carvings and paintings on her temple walls, which still amaze people today.

Building Projects

Hatshepsut was also known for her ambitious building projects. She constructed a stunning temple at Deir el-Bahri, near the Valley of the Kings. This temple, with its elegant terraces and pillars, is considered one of the architectural wonders of ancient Egypt. Its walls tell the story of her divine birth and successful reign.

Her Legacy

Hatshepsut's success as a pharaoh was so profound that after her death, attempts were made to erase her from history. Her successor, Thutmose III, might have felt overshadowed by her achievements and ordered her images and name to be removed from temples and monuments. But despite these efforts, Hatshepsut's legacy endured. Modern archaeologists and historians have pieced together her story, and she is now recognized as one of Egypt's most successful and intriguing rulers.

Hatshepsut's story teaches us about the courage to defy expectations. She shows us that leadership and wisdom are not bound by gender. Hatshepsut took on the role of pharaoh not just to wield power, but to serve her people and guide her country to prosperity. Her story is a powerful reminder that with determination and intelligence, anyone can achieve greatness, no matter the obstacles. Hatshepsut not only carved her monuments into the stone of Egypt but also her legacy into the history of its great rulers.

Sobekneferu: The First Confirmed Female Pharaoh

Hatshepsut was not the only woman from ancient Egypt who was remarkable. Our next character's name was Sobekneferu, who became the first confirmed female pharaoh of Egypt. Her story is not just about ruling a kingdom but also about breaking down barriers and setting a precedent for future generations.

Sobekneferu, whose name means "the beauty of Sobek," was the daughter of Pharaoh Amenemhat III, who was one of the great rulers of the Twelfth Dynasty. After the death of her brother, there were no other male heirs to take the throne, so

Sobekneferu stepped forward to lead Egypt. She thus became Egypt's first known female pharaoh.

Becoming Pharaoh

Imagine a time when most rulers were men, but along came Sobekneferu, a princess with the courage to become a queen and then a pharaoh. When she took the throne, she faced the enormous task of leading one of the most powerful and sophisticated civilizations in the world. Sobekneferu not only took on this role but also embraced it fully, using both traditional and innovative ways to show that she was a capable ruler.

Though Sobekneferu ruled Egypt for almost four years, which was a relatively short time, her impact was significant. She continued the building projects started by her father, showing her skills in maintaining the prosperity and stability of the kingdom. Her reign demonstrated her ability to govern a nation, manage extensive architectural projects, and uphold religious traditions, which were critical aspects of being a pharaoh.

Symbols of Power

To assert her authority, Sobekneferu used many of the same symbols and titles as male pharaohs. She wore the traditional false beard, which was a symbol of pharaonic power. Her statues were also made to show her both in female and traditional male pharaoh attire. This blending of gender symbols in representations of Sobekneferu showed her subjects that she possessed all the qualities needed to rule Egypt, regardless of her gender.

The Legacy of Sobekneferu

Although Sobekneferu's reign was brief, she opened the door for other women to rule Egypt. The most famous of these was Cleopatra, who would rule about 1,400 years later. Sobekneferu proved that a woman could take on the role of pharaoh and lead with strength and wisdom. Her legacy exists not only in what she built with stone, but also in the ideas she cemented about leadership.

Sobekneferu shows us that history is full of pioneers, or people who dare to do things differently and challenge the norms of their times. Her story is a lesson in bravery and the ability to lead in the face of uncertainty. It teaches us that leadership is not about gender but about the courage to stand up and take responsibility when it is needed most.

Sobekneferu's Influence on History

Today, when we talk about Sobekneferu, we remember her not only as a pharaoh but as a trailblazer who helped to redefine possibilities for women in power. She is an inspiration to all of us, showing that you can be a leader by being yourself and embracing the roles you choose to take on.

So, as we turn the pages of history books and uncover the stories of great leaders, let us remember Sobekneferu, the first confirmed female pharaoh of Egypt. Her reign may have been short, but her impact on history was monumental. She teaches us that sometimes, it's not the length of time we have but what we do with it that truly counts.

Queen Nitocris: The Legendary Ruler of the Nile

Let's move from the iconic Sobekneferu to the puzzling and enigmatic Queen Nitocris.. While some scholars debate her very existence, arguing she may have been a mythical or symbolic figure, other ancient texts mention that she was a real ruler. She is often remembered as a fair and wise leader who ascended to the throne under dramatic circumstances—following the untimely death of her brother, the last pharaoh of their dynasty.

Her Rule and Reign

Legend has it that Nitocris was more than just a ruler; she was also a reformer who brought prosperity back to a faltering Egypt. Her reign was marked by a series of bold initiatives intended to restore the stability and richness of her kingdom. It's said that she ruled with both wisdom and benevolence, implementing policies that improved the lives of her people and ensured the kingdom's prosperity.

Architectural Achievements

Queen Nitocris is credited with several ambitious architectural projects that showcased her foresight and brilliance in engineering. Among these were the construction of dams and canals that helped control the flooding of the Nile. These projects were crucial for improving irrigation (making water accessible for crops) and agriculture, which were the backbone of Egypt's economy. Additionally, she strengthened Egypt's defenses, preparing the kingdom against potential invasions.

A Reputation for Justice

One of the most enduring aspects of Nitocris's legacy is her commitment to justice. She is said to have been a fair and strict ruler, creating laws that ensured order and fairness within her kingdom. Her wisdom and fairness earned her the respect and admiration of her subjects.

Her Mysterious Legacy

Despite the tales of her great deeds, concrete historical evidence of Nitocris's reign has not been discovered. This lack of definitive records has fueled ongoing debates among historians and archaeologists (people who study humans and societies) about whether she existed. Some suggest that Nitocris may have represented a combination of the qualities and achievements of several lesser-known female rulers of her time.

Regardless of the debates surrounding her existence, the story of Queen Nitocris has left a lasting mark on Egyptian folklore and the narrative of ancient civilizations. She is a symbol of female empowerment and leadership, inspiring tales and scholarly discussions that span centuries. Like Sobekneferu and Hatshepsut, Queen Nitocris's legend proves that women in ancient governments could have an impact in societies traditionally dominated by men.

Queen Nitocris's legendary wisdom and just rule remains a fascinating subject in the study of ancient Egypt. Whether she walked the earth as a pharaoh or sprang from the imagination of later generations, her story encourages us to think about the roles women played in ancient history and the legends we still remember.

Tiy: The Powerful Matriarch

Though Queen Nitocris may have been a real queen or just the combination of many less influential but equally important female rulers, our next character, Tiy, was a real and powerful matriarch whose wisdom and influence shaped the future of Egypt. Let's dive into the incredible life of Queen Tiy and learn how she became one of the most influential figures in Egyptian history.

Queen Tiy was the wife of Pharaoh Amenhotep III and the mother of Akhenaten (who worshiped only the sun god), one of Egypt's most controversial pharaohs. She was not from a royal background, which makes her rise to prominence even more remarkable. Tiy was not only a queen but a true partner to her husband, involved deeply in the political and cultural life of Egypt.

A Queen with Many Roles

Unlike many other queens of her time, Tiy was depicted almost as an equal to her husband in statues and paintings, which was quite rare in ancient Egypt. This proves that she was both respected and powerful. She wore crowns and headdresses that usually only pharaohs could use and was often shown participating in ceremonies and important state functions.

Queen Tiy was known for her sharp mind and political skills. She played a significant role in maintaining relationships with other powerful kingdoms. Letters between Queen Tiy and foreign dignitaries have been found, meaning she was actively involved in Egypt's foreign affairs. This would have normally been a task reserved for the pharaoh himself.

Mother of a Revolutionary

As the mother of Akhenaten, Queen Tiy had a significant influence on her son, who would go on to challenge Egypt's traditional religious beliefs through his worship of one god over many. Her guidance and support were crucial as her son navigated these radical ideas, which also reshaped Egyptian religion and art.

Queen Tiy was so loved and respected that her husband, Amenhotep III, built several temples and statues in her honor. This was quite unusual for a queen at the time. One of the most famous statues of Queen Tiy, which can be seen in museums today, shows her with a serene yet strong face, wearing a tight-fitting gown and a heavy wig decorated with a floral diadem (a special headband that showed the importance of the person wearing it).

Legacy in Art and Culture

Tiy's legacy is also found in the art of her time. Both her and her family's influence caused a shift in Egyptian art towards realism. The artistic styles developed during her time set the stage for what would come during her son's reign. Her impact on Egyptian art and culture was profound, setting trends that would continue for generations.

Queen Tiy's story teaches us about the power of influence and intelligence. As a matriarch, she shows that leadership comes in many forms—for example, in guiding a family, advising a ruler, or managing a kingdom's most important relationships. Her life reminds us that behind every great leader are advisors and family members who play crucial roles in their decisions and lives.

Tiy's Influence on History

Tiy was a queen who stood out not because she sought power, but because she wielded her influence with wisdom and kindness. She supported her husband and son, managed her family's legacy, and contributed to the prosperity of her nation. Her story is a testament to the important roles women have played throughout history as leaders and pioneers.

So, as we look back at the tales of ancient Egypt, let's remember Queen Tiy. Do not remember her as just a queen, but as a matriarch who used her position to guide her family through times of transformation. She shows us that being a leader isn't just about having power; it's about how you help others and make a lasting impact.

Cleopatra: The Last Queen and Her Roman Ties

Long ago, in the ancient land of Egypt, there lived a queen with a story so fascinating that people still talk about her today. Her name was Cleopatra VII, the last queen of Egypt. Cleopatra was not just a ruler; she was also a scholar, a diplomat, and a savvy political strategist. Her life was full of drama, romance, and intrigue, especially when related to the mighty Roman Empire.

Who Was Cleopatra?

Cleopatra was born into the Ptolemaic dynasty, a family that came from Greece but ruled Egypt for many centuries. She became queen at the young age of 18. Right from the start, it was clear that Cleopatra had big plans for her kingdom. Unlike other rulers of her time, she was also known for being incredibly smart; she spoke many languages and was educated in mathematics, philosophy, and astronomy.

Cleopatra's Roman Connections

Cleopatra's reign was marked by her close ties with Rome, the superpower of her time. She knew that keeping a good relationship with Rome was key to keeping her throne. This led to famous alliances between Egypt and some of the most powerful Roman leaders.

Julius Caesar

The first of these famous Roman leaders was Julius Caesar, a mighty Roman general. Cleopatra met him when she was in a bit of a pickle because she was fighting her brother for control of Egypt. Cleopatra had herself wrapped in a rug (though say it was a sack) and smuggled into Caesar's presence to ask for his help. Caesar was charmed by the young queen's bravery and intelligence, so he helped her regain her throne. Thus, during Caesar's stay in Egypt, they became allies and even had a son together named Caesarion.

Mark Antony

After Caesar was tragically killed, Cleopatra found another Roman ally in Mark Antony, a dashing Roman leader. Theirs is one of the greatest love stories ever told. Antony and Cleopatra fell deeply in love, causing Antony to spend a winter in Egypt. This period was known as the Winter of Discontent due to the great political tensions in Rome caused by their union. Still, they had three children together and dreamed of creating a new empire that would combine the powers of Rome and Egypt.

However, not everyone in Rome liked the idea of a Roman leader teaming up with an Egyptian queen. Antony's rival, Octavian (who would later become Emperor Augustus), used their relationship to stir up trouble in Rome. This rivalry led to a great naval battle at Actium, where Cleopatra and Antony were defeated.

The End of an Era

After their defeat, Antony and Cleopatra returned to Egypt. Knowing that they could not win against Octavian, they both chose to end their own lives.

Antony fell on his sword, and Cleopatra, ever the queen, was bitten by a venomous snake.

Why Cleopatra is Remembered

Cleopatra was the last pharaoh of Egypt. Her death marked the end of Egyptian rule and the beginning of Roman control over Egypt. But, Cleopatra's legacy isn't just about how she died; it's also about how she lived. She was a ruler who used her intelligence, charm, and political savvy to try to restore Egypt to greatness.

Cleopatra's story shows us that history is not just about battles and territories, but also about the power of personality and the impact one person can have on the world around them. We can learn about the importance of courage and determination from Cleopatra's story. Her life as a leader, mother, and scholar continues to inspire people around the world today.

Chapter Conclusion

These remarkable Egyptian queens ruled over the sun-drenched land of ancient Egypt, amidst the grandeur of pyramids and the mystique of the Nile, with dignity, strength, and wisdom. As we draw the curtains on this captivating chapter, we reflect on the profound impact these remarkable women had on history and their legacy.

From the splendor of Nefertiti's court to the intrigue of Cleopatra's alliances, each queen's story offers a window into an ancient kingdom, where power and influence were wielded both gracefully and cunningly. Their reigns were marked by innovation, diplomacy, and the pursuit of greatness.

But beyond the glitz and glamor of the royal court, the queens of the Nile also embodied timeless virtues that transcend centuries. They exemplified courage, wisdom in times of uncertainty, and compassion for their people's welfare. Theirs were tales of resilience, determination, and unwavering resolve, inspiring generations to come.

As we bid farewell to these magnificent queens, let us carry their legacy forward by honoring their memory and embracing the timeless ideals they embodied. May their stories serve as inspiration for all who dare to dream. Let these rulers also remind us that the spirit of queenship lives on in the hearts of all those who dare to lead with the same grace and dignity.

CHAPTER 3:
THE MYSTERIOUS MUMMIES

Before we dive into the fascinating world of mummification, let's take a moment to imagine how ancient Egyptians would have felt and what they believed—Egypt was a place where everyday things were filled with special meaning, and where people believed in magic and mystery. So, in this ancient land, when someone passed away, it wasn't the end of their story but the start of a new adventure.

Picture yourself by the great Nile River, surrounded by towering pyramids and golden temples. Here, the ancient Egyptians had a unique way of preparing their loved ones for the afterlife. They didn't just bury them in the ground; they turned them into mummies—bodies that stayed preserved for thousands of years.

Mummies were preserved so they wouldn't rot or decompose like a normal body would. To follow this method of preservation, the Egyptians used special salts and wrapped the body in linen.

Why Did Egyptians Make Mummies?

You might be thinking, "Why would anyone want to keep old bodies around?" Well, for the ancient Egyptians, making someone into a mummy was very important because they believed in life after death. They believed that when you die, your spirit goes on a journey to another world, where it can live forever in happiness. But there's a catch! To reach this wonderful afterlife, the spirit needed its body. That's why they preserved the bodies, so the spirit could recognize and use it in the next world.

The Mummification Process: A Step-by-Step Adventure

Imagine you are an ancient Egyptian embalmer, a special kind of "magician" who turns people into mummies. Here's what you would do:

- **The Purification**: First, you would clean the body with a palm wine (which smells great) and rinse it with Nile water. It's similar to preparing the body for a royal bath!
- **Removing the Insides**: Next, you would carefully take out the stomach, intestines, lungs, and liver. Don't worry; they didn't throw these away! They preserved these in

special jars called "canopic jars," and each one was protected by a god.

- **Taking Care of the Heart:** The heart was believed to be a human's center of thought and emotion, so that was left inside the body. Egyptians thought it would be needed in the afterlife to help when the gods judged the deceased.
- **Drying Out the Body:** After removing the other organs (and leaving the heart alone), you would use a special salt called "natron" and pack it around the body. This salt dried out the body completely, which took about 40 days. This step stopped the body from rotting.
- **Wrapping Up:** After the body was fully dried, you would wrap it in hundreds of yards of linen strips, almost like bandages. Sometimes, embalmers placed amulets or small magical charms between the layers for protection on the journey to the afterlife.
- **The Final Touches:** Finally, you would place the mummy in a decorated coffin. This meant the mummy was ready to be taken to its tomb, which served as a safe house for the mummy where it could rest peacefully and the person's spirit could enjoy the afterlife.

So Why All The Effort?

Egyptians went through all this trouble because they believed that mummification was a way to keep the person alive in the world of the gods. Becoming a mummy was their ticket to eternity, ensuring that person would continue to exist and enjoy the pleasures of life after death. Every step in the process of mummification was filled with care, respect, and lots of magic spells to protect the deceased on their journey to the afterlife.

From Mummies to Mysteries: Exploring Egyptian Tombs

Now that we understand how and why the ancient Egyptians preserved their dead, let's take the next step to experience the incredible structures built to house these mummies—their tombs. Grab your explorer hats and flashlights, because we're about to go on a thrilling journey. Imagine being an archaeologist, which you could compare to being a type of treasure hunter. You must dig through the sands of time to discover secrets hidden for thousands of years. What treasures and tales lie within these sacred spaces? Let's see what these tomb explorers have found inside!

What is a Tomb?

First, let's talk about what a tomb really is. In ancient Egypt, a tomb was not just a grave (or a place to bury bodies); it was a house for the afterlife. The Egyptians believed that when you died, you went on to live in another world where you would need all the things you had and enjoyed while you were alive. So, they built tombs to be safe places where they could keep the person's treasures, favorite snacks, and even their beds!

The Discovery of Tombs

Archaeologists are not only treasure hunters, because they also act like detectives. They use clues from old writings and the landscape to find where the tombs are hidden. Most of these tombs are found in special places called "necropolises," which are like cities for the dead. These cities are often located in the desert, where the dry sand helps keep everything inside the tombs safe and sound for thousands of years.

Inside the Tombs

When archaeologists first enter a tomb, they find passages that lead to different rooms, just like in a house. These rooms are filled with amazing things:

- **Mummies**: Of course, the most important thing in a tomb is the mummy lying in its coffin, which is often decorated with gold and colorful pictures that tell stories about the person's life.
- **Treasures**: Tombs can be treasure chests filled with gold, jewelry, and precious stones. These were not just to show off, but to help the person in the afterlife. Egyptians believed gold was the skin of the gods!
- **Wall Paintings and Carvings**: The walls of tombs are covered with paintings and

carvings as well. These are not just decorations, as they tell stories of the person's life. These images show the person hunting, fishing, and partying with their family. They also include spells from the Book of the Dead to help them in the afterlife.
- **Daily Life Items:** Imagine finding toys, clothes, furniture, and even makeup in a tomb. Egyptians included these small belongings so the person in the tomb could use them forever.
- **Food and Drink**: Egyptians also included pots of beer, wine, bread, and meat in tombs. Why? Because even after death, Egyptians wanted to feast!

Famous Tomb Discoveries

Remember King Tut? His tomb was one of the most famous discoveries of archaeologists. His tomb was found almost untouched in 1922 by the archaeologist Howard Carter. Inside, there were over 5,000 items, including a golden throne, a chariot, and even King Tut's sandals! His coffin was made of solid gold, and his mask is one of the most famous treasures in the world.

The Mystery and Magic of Tombs

Every time a tomb is discovered, it's like opening a time capsule. These tombs help us understand how the ancient Egyptians lived, what they believed, and how they saw the world. These Discoveries are not just about finding gold or mummies; they're also about uncovering stories from the past.

Why Are These Discoveries Important?

Finding these tombs teaches us more than just history; it shows us the creativity and beliefs of ancient people. It helps us see that even though cultures are different, we all share similar dreams and hopes. It connects us to the past and teaches us to respect other ways of life. Each tomb is like a puzzle box waiting to be solved, full of history, treasures, and tales of old. There are still many tombs hidden under the sands, waiting for the next generation of archaeologists—maybe even you—to uncover their secrets.

As we continue our exploration, we now turn to a fundamental question that has guided much of ancient Egyptian spiritual and practical life; what did the Egyptians believe about the life that awaited them after death?

The Afterlife

Having uncovered the treasures and secrets within ancient Egyptian tombs, let's delve deeper into one of Egypt's most fascinating beliefs; the afterlife. The reason that Egyptians made mummies in the first place ties back to their hopes and dreams for life after death. Join us as we unravel this ancient mystery and learn about the spiritual beliefs that shaped an entire civilization!

What is the Afterlife?

Imagine a place where you could do all your favorite things forever. No school, no chores—just fun, games, and feasts! The ancient Egyptians believed that such a place existed. They thought that after they died, they would go on to live in this wonderful world as long as they did.

Why Make a Mummy?

To the Egyptians, the body was a home for the soul. So, if the body was damaged or disappeared, the soul might get lost and therefore never reach the afterlife. That would be a disaster! So, they developed mummification to keep the body safe and intact. Making a mummy was like packing a suitcase for a long trip, ensuring you had everything you needed to travel to the afterlife.

The Journey to the Afterlife

The Egyptians believed that the journey to the afterlife was full of challenges and adventures. To help the deceased on their way, they included spells and magical items with the mummy. As previously mentioned, one famous collection of spells is known as the "Book of the Dead." These spells were like a map that helped the soul navigate the tricky parts of their journey.

The Fields of Reeds

So how did the Egyptians imagine the afterlife? They pictured it as a lush and beautiful place called the Fields of Reeds. They thought it looked a bit like the best parts of Egypt—full of green fields, flowing rivers, and lots of food. In this heavenly place, people would do the things they loved, like fishing, farming, and feasting, all day long.

Judgement Day

But, getting into the Fields of Reeds wasn't easy. The Egyptians believed that you had to pass a test called the "Weighing of the Heart." On this day, the god of the dead, Osiris, and some other gods would judge the deceased. Together they would weigh the person's heart on a giant scale against a feather, which represented truth and justice. If your heart was as light as the feather, it meant that you had lived a good life and could enter the afterlife. But if your heart was heavy with bad deeds, a terrifying creature called Ammit would gobble it up, and you would vanish forever!

Preparing for Eternity

Because the afterlife was so important, Egyptians spent a lot of time and effort preparing for it. They filled their tombs with food, tools, and even statues called "shabtis" that could come to life and work for them in the afterlife. The richer and more powerful you were, the bigger and more elaborate your tomb would be. So, naturally the pharaohs' tombs were massive pyramids.

What an amazing belief system, right? As we close this chapter, think about the incredible lengths the Egyptians went to in order to secure their eternal happiness.

But our journey through the mysteries of ancient Egypt is far from over. There are still countless secrets waiting to be unearthed, stories waiting to be told. So, as we conclude this chapter, let's keep our explorer spirit alive and ready for the adventures that lie ahead. Who knows what wonders we'll discover next in the timeless sands of Egypt's past?

EGYPTIAN LEGENDS FOR KIDS

CHAPTER 4: GODS AND GODDESSES

Welcome to a new chapter of our journey through ancient Egypt! In this chapter, we'll dive into the exciting world of Egyptian gods and goddesses. These divine beings were super important to the ancient Egyptians. They were like important celebrities, but with special powers!

Imagine a world where gods and goddesses ruled the sky, the earth, and everything in between. That's ancient Egypt! The Egyptians believed in many gods and goddesses, each with their own jobs and superpowers. These gods were like big stars in the sky, and people looked up to them for help and protection.

Religion was a big deal in ancient Egypt. For them, it was more than going to temples and saying prayers; in fact, it was a way of life. The Egyptians believed in balance, and felt it was the gods who made sure the sun rose every day and the crops grew well. They thought that if they pleased the gods, everything would go smoothly.

Each god and goddess had a special job to do. For example, Ra was the sun god, so he made sure the world had light and warmth every day. Osiris looked after the dead, guiding them to the afterlife. And Hathor brought joy and happiness to everyone she met. These gods and goddesses were like superheroes, each with their own powers and responsibilities.

As we learn about the gods and goddesses of ancient Egypt, we're not just exploring stories from the past; we're discovering important lessons about kindness, bravery, and the wonders of the world. So get ready to journey back in time and uncover the secrets of Egypt's magical pantheon!

Ra: The Sun God

Ra is one of the most important and powerful gods in ancient Egyptian mythology. Because he is the god of the sun, his job was a big deal because the sun is very important—it provides light, warmth, and life to the whole world. The Egyptians believed that every morning, Ra's golden sun chariot rose in the east, traveled across the sky, and set in the west. Egyptians believed that Ra's journey brought daylight to the world and that he defeated darkness every day.

The Look of a Sun God

Imagine a god with the head of a falcon and a sun disk resting on his head. That's Ra! This sun disk was a powerful symbol glowing with fiery light, and showed that Ra was the king of all gods. His falcon head, sharp and majestic, helped him watch over the world from high above, making sure everything was in order.

Ra's Daily Journey

Each day was an epic adventure for Ra. His job was to drive the sun across the sky in his magical chariot. But it wasn't a peaceful trip; Ra had to fight off the monster of chaos, Apophis, who was a giant snake that tried to swallow the sun every night. This battle happened in the underworld, the mysterious realm below the earth, during the night. By winning this fight every night, Ra made sure that the sun would rise again the next day, bringing light and life back to the world.

Ra and the Creation of the World

Ra was not just the god of the sun; he was also a creator of the world (according to one ancient story)!! It all started when Ra spoke the names of things, and poof! They came into being. He named the mountains, the seas, the plants, animals, and even humans. This story shows just how powerful words and names were to the ancient Egyptians.

Ra's Family

Ra was at the center of a big family of gods and goddesses. He was thought to be the father of many gods, but his most famous children are Shu, the god of air, and Tefnut, the goddess of moisture. These two gods represented how essential air and water are for life, also demonstrating that Ra's power extended to all parts of creation.

The Temples and Worship of Ra

The Egyptians built great temples to honor Ra, and people worshiped him through music, singing, and celebrations. The priests at these temples performed daily rituals to help keep Ra strong in his battle against chaos. They offered him beautiful prayers, sang hymns, and presented offerings of food and treasures. They believed these rituals were very important to keep the universe in balance and ensure that Ra continued his journey across the sky each day.

The Legend of Ra's Secret Name

One of the most fascinating tales about Ra is about his secret name. It was believed that Ra had a hidden name that held all his power. If anyone ever learned this secret name, they would have control over Ra and his powers. Legend has it that the clever goddess, Isis, wanted to know this secret name. Through a clever trick, she managed to learn it from Ra, gaining immense wisdom and power.

Why Ra Matters

Ra was more than just a sun god to the Egyptians; he was a symbol of life, order, and power. By understanding Ra, we get a glimpse into how the ancient Egyptians saw the world. They saw the universe as a beautiful, ordered place where every day was a victory of light over darkness, and life over chaos.

Anubis: Guardian of the Underworld

Now let's imagine another god with the body of a man and the head of a sleek, black jackal (an animal related to dogs). That's Anubis! In ancient Egyptian mythology, Anubis is known as the God of Mummification and the Afterlife.

The Role of Anubis

Anubis had a very important job. He was the protector of the dead, making sure they were safe on their journey to the afterlife. But his duties didn't stop there. Anubis was also in charge of mummification—the special process of preserving bodies to make mummies as we talked about in the previous chapter. Imagine him as a divine embalmer, ensuring that the mummies were ready for their eternal life.

The Ceremony of Mummification

Anubis was the master of ceremonies when it came to mummification. He watched over the embalmers' work, guiding their hands as they prepared the body. Once the body was wrapped up as a mummy, Anubis performed the "Opening of the Mouth" ceremony. This ritual was believed to bring the mummy back to life so it could eat, drink, and speak in the afterlife.

Anubis and the Weighing of the Heart

One of the most thrilling moments in the journey to the afterlife was the Weighing of the Heart ceremony, and Anubis played a starring role. In the great Hall of Maat, Anubis would place the heart of the deceased on the giant scale that was only balanced with a feather.

If the heart was lighter than the feather, it meant the person had led a good life and could go on to the paradise of the afterlife. But if the heart was heavier, it was eaten by Ammit and their soul would disappear forever.

Why a Jackal Head?

You might be wondering, why did Anubis have a jackal head? Well, jackals were common in the deserts around Egypt, often seen lurking around cemeteries at night. The Egyptians thought that Anubis, in the form of a jackal, was protecting the dead. So, Anubis's jackal head is a sign of his role as a protector and guardian.

Temples and Worship

While Anubis was a very popular god, he didn't have as many temples dedicated to him as some of the other gods. Instead, places where mummification and rituals for the dead were carried out were considered his sacred spaces. People would also offer prayers and gifts to Anubis to ask for his protection for their loved ones who had passed away.

Anubis's Legacy

Anubis is one of the coolest and most unique gods in Egyptian mythology. His appearance captures our imagination and takes us back to a time when people saw the world in a magical way. He helps us understand how the ancient Egyptians felt about death and the afterlife—it wasn't something to be scared of, but a journey to be prepared for. Anubis was the guardian watching over it all.

Anubis shows us the importance of caring for those who have passed and protecting them on their way to the next life. As we continue our journey through the legends about the Gods And Goddesses of Egypt, keep the image of Anubis in your mind—the kind and powerful protector who watches over the night.

Osiris: Ruler of the Dead

After discussing the guardian of the dead, let's move onto their ruler, Osiris. Osiris was one of the most important gods in ancient Egyptian mythology. He was the god of the afterlife, the underworld, and rebirth. Imagine him as the king who looks after everyone who has passed away, making sure they have a safe journey in the world beyond. Osiris is often shown as a mummy holding a crook and flail (symbols of kingship). He has distinctive green or black skin, which represents rebirth and the fertile Nile soil.

The Story of Osiris

The story of Osiris is a tale of jealousy, betrayal, and the power of love. Osiris was a beloved king of Egypt who taught the people how to farm and make laws. His brother, Set, was jealous of his power and popularity. In a wicked plot, Set tricked Osiris by offering him a beautiful chest at a banquet. He said he would give the chest to anyone who could fit perfectly inside it. When Osiris lay down in the chest, Set slammed it shut, sealed it, and threw it into the Nile River.

But the story doesn't end there! Osiris's wife, Isis, who was a powerful goddess herself, searched everywhere for her husband. She found his chest and brought it back to Egypt. Sadly, Set found the chest again, stole Osiris's body, and chopped it into pieces, scattering them across Egypt. The determined Isis gathered all the pieces, and with her magic, brought Osiris back to life long enough to conceive their son, Horus. Afterward, Osiris became the god of the underworld, ruling over the dead and offering them the chance of rebirth.

Osiris and the Afterlife

As the Ruler of the Dead, Osiris's job was to welcome the souls into the underworld. Here, he would judge them in the Hall of Truth. As previously mentioned, in this mystical room the hearts of the dead were weighed against the feather of Maat, the goddess of truth and justice.

Celebrating Osiris

Osiris was not only the god of death but also of resurrection and life. Every year, the Egyptians celebrated the mysteries of Osiris. These were special ceremonies that reenacted the story of his death and rebirth. They believed these rituals would renew the fertility of the land and help the dead be reborn in the afterlife. Villages across Egypt had their own versions of these rituals, showing just how beloved and central Osiris was in their lives.

Osiris's Influence

Osiris had a huge impact on Egyptian culture. He was a symbol of hope, promising a peaceful and blessed existence in the afterlife for those who lived a virtuous life. His story encouraged the people to follow the values of truth and righteousness.

Osiris's tale teaches us about the values that were important to the ancient Egyptians—justice, truth, and loyalty. As the Ruler of the Dead, Osiris reassures us that there is always a chance for renewal and rebirth, no matter the challenges we face. So, as we close this chapter on Osiris, remember the lessons he brings: that goodness and justice can triumph over evil, and that love and determination can overcome any obstacle.

Isis: Goddess of Magic

Now let's talk about Osiris's wife, Isis, who was a goddess that could do it all. She was known as the goddess of magic, motherhood, healing, and even the protector of the kingdom. Egyptians pictured her as a beautiful woman wearing a throne-shaped crown, because she was also considered the queen of the gods. Her powerful wings could spread far and wide to protect those in need.

The Story of Isis

The story of Isis is one of adventure, love, and magic. Because Isis was married to Osiris, who was originally the king of Egypt, they ruled the land together. But when Osiris was betrayed and killed by his jealous brother, Set, the kingdom fell into darkness. However, like mentioned in the previous section, Isis gathered the pieces of her husband's body and used her magic to bring him back to life.

Isis also used her wits and magic to protect her son, Horus, from Set. She raised Horus in secret swamps and marshes where Set couldn't find them. With her guidance, Horus grew strong and wise, and he eventually defeated Set. Horus thus became the new king of Egypt. So, Isis's magic and cleverness were key to restoring balance and peace.

Isis's Magical Powers

Isis was known for her incredible magical abilities. She could heal the sick, protect the dead, and even control the fate of the skies. One of her most famous tales involves tricking the sun god Ra. Remember that Ra was very powerful and had a secret name that held the source of his strength. Using her wits, Isis crafted a snake from the earth that bit Ra. After the snake had bit him, Isis offered to heal him if he told her his secret name. Ra eventually gave in, meaning that Isis gained even more magical powers.

The Worship of Isis

Isis was worshiped all over Egypt and even beyond its borders. She had many temples dedicated to her, where people would come to ask for her blessings and protection. The priests and priestesses who served her performed rituals to harness her magical powers, hoping to bring healing and protection to their communities. The festival of Isis was also a grand celebration connected to the Nile flooding, which was a crucial event for farming. People thanked Isis during this festival for bringing fertility and life to their fields.

Isis's Legacy

The influence of Isis spread far beyond the sands of Egypt. After the time of the pharaohs, people in the Roman Empire and beyond worshiped her. She became a symbol of the ideal mother and wife, as well as a protector of nature and the people. Her image has inspired countless generations, and her stories continue to fascinate people around the world.

Isis, the Goddess of Magic, shows us the power of love, protection, and clever thinking. Her magical adventures and caring nature teach us about the strength that comes from caring for others and standing up for what's right. As we close this chapter, remember Isis as a symbol of the magical possibilities all around us.

Horus: The Falcon God of Protection

Horus is one of the most important gods in ancient Egyptian mythology. He's usually shown as a man with the head of a falcon that wears a crown with red and white colors, which represent Egypt. As the god of the sky, Horus's eyes are literally the sun and moon, where the sun occupies his right eye and the moon his left. Imagine having the whole sky as your kingdom!

The Birth of Horus

Horus's story begins with his parents, Isis and Osiris. After Osiris was betrayed by Set, Isis used her magical powers to bring Osiris back to life long enough to conceive Horus. Horus was born in secret, hidden in the marshes of the Nile Delta to keep him safe from Set, who wanted to prevent him from claiming the throne.

Horus's Battle for the Throne

As Horus grew, he was determined to avenge his father's death and reclaim the throne from Set. This led to a series of epic battles between Horus and Set, which are among the most famous stories in Egyptian mythology. These battles were not just physical fights but also involved clever tricks and magical contests. In the end, with the help of the other gods, Horus won, and he became the ruler of Egypt, symbolizing the triumph of good over evil.

Horus as the God of Protection

As the ruler of Egypt, Horus had a very special role: he was the protector of the pharaohs. The pharaohs were considered to be the 'living Horuses,' meaning they were earthly embodiments of the god himself. This is why you often see statues and images of Horus standing behind a pharaoh, spreading his wings protectively. It was believed that Horus watched over the pharaohs as their divine guardian, ensuring they had the wisdom and strength to rule wisely.

The Eye of Horus

One of the most famous symbols associated with Horus is the "Eye of Horus," also known as the "wedjat eye." It's a symbol that looks a bit like a stylized eye with a twisty tail coming out of it. This symbol was a powerful amulet used for protection against evil and illness. It was worn by the living and placed on the dead to protect them during their journey through the underworld.

The Worship of Horus

Temples dedicated to Horus dotted the landscape of ancient Egypt. The most famous temple was the Temple of Horus at Edfu, which also happens to be one of the most well-preserved temples in all of Egypt. Inside, walls adorned with carvings tell the story of Horus's epic battles and his victory over Set. Priests in these temples performed daily rituals to honor Horus, asking for his protection and favor.

Horus's Legacy

Horus remained one of the most significant gods in ancient Egyptian religion throughout the history of the civilization. His image as a falcon-headed man represents strength, vigilance, and the rule of law, all of which were central values to the ancient Egyptians. His connection to the pharaohs also underscored the divine right to rule that was vital to maintaining order and stability in ancient Egyptian society.

Horus teaches us about courage, justice, and the protective power of leadership. As we continue our journey through Egyptian Legends, keep your eyes on the sky—maybe you'll spot Horus watching over you too!

Set: God of Chaos and Disorder

Though he might sound a bit scary, Set's story is full of wild adventures. So, let's find out why Set is one of the most fascinating characters in ancient Egyptian mythology!

Set is a god with a look as unique as his role in Egyptian myths. He's often shown with an animal head that's hard to identify—it looks a bit like an aardvark, a donkey, and a jackal all mixed together! This mysterious animal is called the "Set animal" and it's just as wild and unpredictable as Set himself. Set was the god of chaos, storms, and war. But even though he represents chaos, Set also played a crucial part in protecting the sun god, Ra, from his nightly battles against the serpent Apophis.

Protector of the Sun God

Despite his reputation for chaos and disruption, Set was not just a villain. He had a very important job every night as one of the protectors of Ra's solar barge. Ra sailed through the underworld each night. Every evening, Set fought against Apophis, a giant serpent who tried to swallow the sun. This battle was crucial because it ensured that the sun rose each morning. In this way, Set's destructive power was also used to protect the world from eternal darkness.

The Worship of Set

Set was worshiped in various parts of ancient Egypt, particularly in places where storms and harsh weather were common. People believed that honoring Set could protect them from natural disasters and help them in battles. His temples were places where people prayed for strength and resilience in the face of chaos.

Set in Egyptian Culture

Even though Set was associated with violence and disorder, he was also a symbol of strength against adversity. The ancient Egyptians understood that chaos and order were two sides of the same coin. They believed both were necessary for the balance of the universe. Set's stories remind us that even in chaos, there is space for structure and protection.

So, young explorers, now you know about Set, the God of Chaos and Disorder. His tales are a mix of thrilling battles, family drama, and the essential balance between order and chaos. Set shows us that every story has many sides and that even a stormy character can display heroism.

Hathor: Goddess of Love and Joy

After exploring the story of the god of chaos, let's meet his opposite, Hathor, the ancient Egyptian

Goddess of Love and Joy. She is one of the most loved and celebrated goddesses from ancient Egypt, and was thought to spread happiness and music wherever she went. So, let's dance along with Hathor and discover her delightful world!

Hathor is depicted as a beautiful woman with the ears of a cow. Sometimes though, she was even depicted as a whole cow. She wore a headdress with horns and a sun disk nestled between them. Why a cow, you might wonder? In ancient Egypt, cows were seen as nurturing animals, providing the essential milk and meat that sustained life. Thus, Hathor's connection with cows symbolizes her role as a nurturing goddess who provides love, protection, and joy to all.

The Many Roles of Hathor

Hathor was known as the goddess of many things—love, beauty, music, dancing, fertility, and motherhood. She was like the ancient version of a superstar, bringing joy and celebration wherever she was worshiped. Hathor's presence was said to bring peace and happiness to homes and temples alike.

The Joyful Protector

Hathor was also a protective goddess. Mothers and children would pray to her for health and happiness. She was especially important to women, who looked up to her as a symbol of femininity and strength. But more than just a protector, people also believed in her power to bring them happiness. So, Hathor's temples were places where music and dance filled the air, creating an atmosphere of joy and festivity.

Hathor and the Sky

One of Hathor's most fascinating roles was as the goddess of the sky. The ancient Egyptians believed she welcomed the rising sun each day with joyous music. She flew around her domain, the sky, as a cow, spreading light and happiness. She was also thought to be the Eye of Ra, meaning she was the sun god's protective female counterpart. As such, she helped Ra fight off enemies and bring the sun across the sky.

Celebrations in Hathor's Honor

The most famous festival celebrated in Hathor's honor was the "Feast of Drunkenness." This might sound strange, but it was actually a joyful and sacred festival! It celebrated a myth in which Hathor, as the Eye of Ra, saved humanity from destruction. People danced, sang, and even drank to excess to imitate and honor the overwhelming joy and love that Hathor brought back to the world after her rage was calmed. It was a way for everyone, from the simplest farmer to the highest priest, to feel connected to the goddess and each other.

Hathor's Temples

Hathor's main temple was at Dendera, which is another one of the most beautiful and well-preserved temples in all of Egypt. This temple was her special home on Earth, and was decorated with magnificent images of her as both a woman and a cow. Pilgrims traveled from far and wide to visit and pay their respects, hoping to gain her favor and enjoy her blessings of joy and love.

Hathor's Legacy

Hathor's legacy is one of love, happiness, and nurturing care. Her stories and the celebrations in her honor show us how the ancient Egyptians cherished and upheld the ideals of love and joy in their culture. Hathor's role goes beyond just myths and legends; she represents the celebration of life itself.

As we finish our chapter on Hathor, the Goddess of Love and Joy, remember that like Hathor, you can bring happiness and love into the lives of those around you. Whether through a smile, a song, or a dance, sharing joy is something that everyone can do, just like Hathor did for the ancient Egyptians.

Thoth: The Wise God of the Moon and Magic

Thoth was her another one of the most important deities in ancient Egyptian mythology. He was often depicted in art as a man with the head of an ibis. An ibis is a type of bird with a long, curved beak. Other times Thoth was depicted with the head of a baboon. Either way, both animals were considered sacred to him. These unique looks made Thoth stand out among the gods and were symbols of his connection to the natural world.

The Roles of Thoth

Thoth wore many hats among the gods. He was not just the god of the moon but also the god of wisdom, knowledge, writing, hieroglyphs, science, magic, art, and judgment. This made him one of the busiest deities on the Egyptian pantheon's payroll!

- **Moon God**: As the god of the Moon, Thoth measured and kept time. The ancient Egyptians believed that Thoth's light in the night sky helped them calculate the days and months.
- **God of Wisdom and Knowledge**: Thoth was believed to hold all the knowledge in the world. He gave the gift of hieroglyphs, which were the Egyptian's system of writing, to humanity. This made him the patron god of scribes (people who wrote or copied books and other texts), who were very respected in ancient Egypt.
- **God of Science and Magic**: Thoth wasn't just about book-smarts; he was also the god of magic and science. As such, he knew secrets that other gods didn't, which made him a powerful figure in myths and capable of solving problems that stumped others.

Thoth's Family

In the rich tapestry of Egyptian mythology, Thoth's feminine counterpart was Seshat, the goddess of writing and measurement. Seshat helped him with his duties. His wife was Ma'at, the goddess of truth and justice, which fit perfectly with his role as a god of wisdom and judgment. Together, they were a powerful pair who maintained the universe's balance and order.

Thoth in Egyptian Art and Culture

Thoth was a popular subject in Egyptian art. He was often shown holding a writing palette and a reed pen, ready to record the deeds of the dead in the underworld—another of his important jobs. This depiction as a record-keeper highlighted his role in the judgment of the dead, where he made sure that justice was carried out correctly.

Thoth's Legacy

Thoth's influence extended beyond just religion; he was a cultural icon that represented the intellectual achievements of ancient Egypt. As such, temples dedicated to Thoth were centers of learning, similar to universities today. His legacy encouraged enlightenment and the pursuit of knowledge.

Thoth teaches us about the value of knowledge and the power of words. His story reminds us that learning and wisdom are treasures that can lead to better understanding and harmony in the world. Thoth's role in Egyptian mythology as a mediator and wise counselor shows us the importance of fair judgment and truth in maintaining order and peace. His fascinating story helps us appreciate the ancient Egyptians' deep respect for knowledge and justice, which are both values that are still important today.

Bastet: The Feline Goddess of Protection

Now let's meet Bastet, the cat goddess. Known for her protective powers and gentle nature, Bastet was a figure that had been worshiped and adored since the Second Dynasty. Let's paw our way into the world of this fascinating goddess.

Bastet, also known as Bast, is an ancient Egyptian goddess who appears as a fierce lioness or a gentle cat. Her names, which include B'sst, Baast, Ubaste, and Baset, reflect her attributes as a deity of home, fertility, and protection. In ancient Greek culture, she was known as Ailuros, meaning "cat."

Bastet was originally depicted as a lioness, which symbolized her role as a protector and warrior. However, over time, her image softened to that of a domestic cat, highlighting her nurturing aspects. This transformation mirrors her dual roles:

- **Protector**: As a fierce lioness, Bastet was seen as a defender of the pharaoh and the nation, warding off enemies and evil spirits. Temples dedicated to Bastet often featured her as a lioness, emphasizing her strength and majesty.
- **Goddess of Home and Fertility**: As a gentle cat, Bastet represented domestic bliss and fertility. She was thought to bring joy and protect homes from evil spirits. Many Egyptian families had statues of Bastet to ensure their household was safe and happy.

Worship of Bastet

Bastet was especially popular in the city of Bubastis, which became her cult center. Here, grand festivals were held in her honor, attracting devotees from across Egypt who came to celebrate her with music, dance, and feasting. The festivals were so lively and joyous that they were famous throughout ancient Egypt.

The Temple of Bastet in Bubastis was one of the most magnificent in all of Egypt. It was a place of pilgrimage and celebration, and people went there to pay homage to the goddess. Archaeologists have found many statues and artifacts in this temple that show how deeply loved and revered Bastet was among the ancient Egyptians.

Bastet and Her Symbolism

The image of Bastet as a cat has a special significance in Egyptian culture. Cats were highly revered animals, valued for their grace and their ability to catch and kill snakes and rats. By associating Bastet with cats, the Egyptians highlighted her protective qualities—she kept away both physical and spiritual vermin that could harm their homes.

The Legacy of Bastet

Today, Bastet is still a symbol of protection and motherly care. Her statues, which show her as both a fierce lioness and a gentle cat, remind us of the dual nature of her powers. She embodies the balance between strength and kindness, which the ancient Egyptians greatly respected. Her story teaches us about the values of protection, joy, and the comforts of home. Bastet's legacy shows us that caring and courage can go hand-in-hand, providing safety and happiness to those we love.

Concluding Our Journey

As we wrap up our exploration of the gods and goddesses of ancient Egypt, we remember the treasure trove of stories, lessons, and wonders we've uncovered. From Ra's journey across the sky to Hathor's joyful celebrations, each deity has left a mark on history and our hearts.

Through the tales of these divine beings, we've learned about the values and beliefs that shaped ancient Egyptian society. We've seen how religion was more than just rituals; it was a guiding force that brought people together and gave meaning to their lives.

But our journey doesn't end here. As we step away from the temples and tombs of ancient Egypt, we carry with us the wisdom left behind by these legends. The lessons of kindness, courage, and the pursuit of knowledge will guide us on our own adventures, helping us navigate the challenges of the modern world.

So let's keep our curiosity alive, always seeking to learn more about the wonders of the past and the mysteries of the universe. Who knows what other ancient secrets are waiting to be uncovered? Remember to keep your hearts open to the magic of history and the beauty of the world around us as we continue into our next chapter.

EGYPTIAN LEGENDS FOR KIDS

CHAPTER 5: MYTHS OF ANCIENT EGYPT

In this chapter, we'll continue our thrilling adventure as we unravel captivating tales that have enchanted people for thousands of years. From the creation of the world to epic battles between gods and monsters, these ancient Egyptian stories are filled with magic, mystery, and timeless wisdom.

Our expedition begins with an introduction to the mythical tales and characters that populate the rich tapestry of Egyptian mythology. These stories not only entertain but also offer insights into the values and beliefs of ancient Egyptian society. As we delve deeper, we'll discover how these myths provide explanations for the natural world and prove to be important moral lessons to generations from the past and present.

The Creation Myth of Heliopolis: Atum and the Ennead

Gather around, young explorers, as we dive into one of the most fascinating tales from ancient Egypt—the Creation Myth of Heliopolis! This story isn't just about how the world began, it's also about the adventures of the god named Atum and his family, known as the Ennead. So, let's set sail on this ancient river of myths and discover how the Egyptians believed the world was created.

The Beginning of Everything

In the very beginning, there was nothing but endless darkness and swirling chaos. This was a silent, empty place called Nun. But within this nothingness, something incredible happened—a mound of land magically appeared! According to the Egyptians, this was the first piece of land ever to exist, and it was called the Benben. On this mound, the first god, Atum, came into being all by himself. Imagine being the first and only one alive in a vast, dark space!

Atum: The First God

Atum was a special god because he possessed the amazing ability of creation. His power meant he was not born the usual way; rather, he created himself out of the chaos. As he stood on Benben, he felt lonely in the endless darkness. So, Atum decided he wanted some company. But how could he create other beings? Well, Atum had a unique way of creating things—by spitting or sneezing! When he did this, he created the first pair of gods—

Shu, the god of air, and Tefnut, the goddess of moisture.

The Adventures of Shu and Tefnut

Shu and Tefnut were the children of Atum. They were very important because they brought air and moisture into the world, which are essential for life. But one day, they wandered off into the darkness and got lost. Atum was so worried about his children that he sent his eye out into the chaos to find them. When Shu and Tefnut finally returned with the eye, Atum was so happy that tears streamed down his face. What's amazing is that where his tears fell, humans sprang up! That's how the first people were created according to this myth.

The Ennead: The Great Family of Gods

As the family grew, Shu and Tefnut had two children of their own—Geb, the god of the earth, and Nut, the goddess of the sky. But their father, Shu, separated his children, as he didn't think the sky should mix with the earth. So, Geb lay below while Nut arched over him, creating the world as the ancient Egyptians knew it.

Geb and Nut also had children—Osiris, Isis, Seth, and Nephthys, who became key figures in many other Egyptian myths. Together, these nine gods (Atum, Shu, Tefnut, Geb, Nut, Osiris, Isis, Seth, and Nephthys) are called the Ennead, which means a group of nine. They were worshiped and loved across Egypt.

Why This Myth Matters

The Creation Myth of Heliopolis explains how the Egyptians understood the world around them. It showed them that even in chaos, there can be order and life, and that families—just like the Ennead—were at the heart of everything. This myth also taught them that everyone and everything has a place in the world, from the air they breathed (Shu) to the ground they walked on (Geb).

So, the story of Atum and the Ennead is just one of the endless wonders of ancient Egypt. Remember, every myth and legend carries a spark of the magic and mystery of the times gone by. As you dream tonight, imagine what it would be like to stand on the first mound of earth and watch a whole world being created!

The Legend of Osiris and Isis: The Story of Resurrection

Now that we've talked about Earth's creation, let's discuss what happened on Earth. We will now revisit the tale of Osiris and Isis in more detail. Remember this story about love, betrayal, and the power of hope? Get ready for a journey into the world of gods, magic, and miracles!

Osiris and Isis were both brother and sister, a husband and wife, which was common for Egyptian gods. They were rulers of the gods and very much in love. Osiris was the god of agriculture and the afterlife, teaching people how to grow crops and live well. Isis was a powerful goddess of magic, known for her wisdom and kindness.

The Jealous Brother

But, not everyone was happy with Osiris. Remember his brother, Set, who was very jealous of Osiris's power and popularity? As we have learned, Set was the god of chaos and the desert. He plotted to take over as the ruler of Egypt.

The Evil Plot

As you already know, Set held a feast and brought a beautiful wooden chest with him. He said that whoever could fit perfectly in the chest would win a competition! All the guests tried their luck, but the chest seemed to fit no one—until Osiris stepped in. As soon as he laid down, Set slammed the lid shut, sealed the chest, and threw it into the Nile River. Remember that Set then declared himself king, and chaos began to spread across Egypt.

The Search for Osiris

We already know that Isis was heartbroken when she learned about Osiris's fate. She couldn't accept his death and set out on a long journey to find him. Her journey led her through many dangers, but her magical powers and determination helped her along the way. Finally, she found the chest containing Osiris's body in a distant land, where it had been caught in a tree's branches.

The Magic of Isis

Isis used her powerful magic to bring Osiris back to life. She breathed new life into Osiris with her wings and spells. For a brief moment, Osiris was alive again, and the two were reunited. Horus was born at this time as well. But Osiris couldn't stay in the world of the living. He became the ruler of the underworld, where he would judge the souls of the dead.

The Birth of Horus and the Revenge

As previously mentioned, Isis hid her son, Horus, in the marshes. She raised Horus to be strong and wise so that he could challenge Set and reclaim his father's throne. The two battled and Horus eventually became the king of Egypt, restoring order and justice.

The Legacy of Osiris and Isis

The story of Osiris and Isis had a huge impact on Egyptian culture. It was a tale of resurrection that promised life after death to ordinary Egyptians, not just the pharaohs and nobles. The promise of being reborn in the afterlife gave them hope and a reason to live a good life according to the laws of Ma'at.

The legend of Osiris and Isis teaches us about the power of love and the enduring nature of the soul.

It shows us that even in the face of the greatest trials, courage and perseverance can restore balance and harmony. Remember, like Isis and Horus, you can overcome challenges with determination and support from those you love.

The Tale of the Shipwrecked Sailor: The Serpent King

After reviewing the epic tale of Horus, Isis, and Osiris, let's move onto distant waters. We start this story with a brave Egyptian sailor who set out on a ship with his fellow crewmen. They were on a mission to find precious treasures for the Pharaoh. The sun was shining, and the sea was calm, but suddenly, a fierce storm came out of nowhere! The winds howled, the waves crashed, and in the chaos, our sailor was thrown overboard.

When the storm finally calmed, the sailor found himself washed up on the shore of a mysterious island. He was all alone, scared, and unsure of what to do next. But he didn't give up. Instead, he started to explore the island, hoping to find food, water, or maybe a way back home.

The Discovery of the Serpent King

As he explored, the sailor stumbled upon a strange and marvelous sight—a huge, shimmering serpent with scales of gold and eyes like the brightest of emeralds. This was no ordinary serpent; it was the Serpent King, a magical creature who ruled over the island. The sailor was terrified at first, but the Serpent King spoke to him in a calm and regal voice, asking him how the sailor came to his island.

The Serpent King's Tale

The Serpent King was not always a serpent. He told the sailor that he used to be a prince of a rich and lush kingdom. But a curse had turned him into a serpent and his subjects vanished, leaving him alone on the island with only his treasures. Despite his fearsome appearance, the Serpent King was kind and wise. He comforted the sailor and promised that no harm would come to him during his stay.

A Promise of Rescue

The Serpent King, moved by the sailor's plight, made a surprising promise. He told the sailor that soon a ship would come to rescue him and take him back to Egypt. Before the sailor's departure, the Serpent King gave him treasures—precious stones and spices—as gifts to take back to his pharaoh. But he also gave a warning: that he couldn't speak of the island to anyone except the pharaoh, for its secrets were not for the ears of ordinary men.

The Return Home

True to the Serpent King's word, a ship arrived. The sailor returned to Egypt with his arms laden with treasures. When he reached home, he went straight to the pharaoh to tell him of all that had happened. The pharaoh was amazed by the story and the riches the sailor brought back. He praised the sailor for his bravery and wisdom in dealing with the Serpent King.

The Lesson of the Tale

The story of the shipwrecked sailor teaches us about courage and kindness in unexpected places. It shows us that even when you feel lost and alone, there can be magical moments and new friends in surprising forms. It's a tale that encourages us to be brave in our adventures and wise in our dealings with the unknown.

The Legendary Adventures of Sphinx

Now from the sea we will move to the sands of Egypt, where a hero known as Sphinx lived. The Sphinx had the body of a lion and the head of a human, making him a powerful and majestic figure. He was revered by all who knew his name. But his strength didn't come from mere muscles—it came from the Orb of Ra, a mystical artifact gifted to him by the ancient god himself.

The Orb of Ra

The Orb of Ra wasn't just any magical object—it was a source of immense power. The Orb was bestowed upon Sphinx to aid him in his quest against darkness. When Sphinx held the orb, he could feel its energy coursing through his veins, filling him with courage and strength. With the orb by his side, Sphinx became the greatest hero Egypt had ever known.

The Quest Against Apep

So, when the land of Egypt was threatened by Apep, a fearsome serpent of chaos who sought to plunge the world into darkness, the Sphinx had to fight. Apep was a formidable foe, with powers that rivaled even the gods themselves. But Sphinx, armed with the Orb of Ra and his unwavering bravery, was determined to stop him.

The Battle of Light and Darkness

The battle between Sphinx and Apep raged across the sands of Egypt, echoing through the ancient temples and pyramids. With every strike of his sword and blast of his magic, Sphinx fought valiantly against the forces of darkness. Apep, however, was cunning and relentless, using his powers to twist the very fabric of reality.

Victory and Triumph

But Sphinx, fueled by the power of the Orb of Ra and his unyielding spirit, refused to back down. With a final, mighty blow, he struck Apep down, banishing the serpent back into the depths of the underworld. The people of Egypt rejoiced, celebrating Sphinx as their savior and protector.

Legacy of Sphinx

Sphinx's victory over Apep became a legend and was retold for generations to come. Temples were built in his honor, and festivals were held in his name, celebrating his bravery and heroism. Sphinx's legacy lived on, inspiring all who heard his story to stand up against darkness and fight for what is right.

And so, dear adventurers, we conclude our tale of Sphinx, the legendary hero of ancient Egypt. Remember, just like Sphinx, each of us has the power to stand up against darkness and make a difference in the world. So, let your courage shine bright, and may your adventures be as legendary as those of Sphinx himself!

The Marvelous Tale of the Ogdoad

Now let's move beyond Egypt's sky and sands to the vast expanse of the universe, to a time before the sun touched the sky or the rivers flowed with life. In this space the Ogdoad existed—the "Eight" who stood at the dawn of creation. These ancient deities existed when the world was but a swirling chaos of darkness and void. It was from their divine essence the cosmos was born.

The Eight Primordial Deities

The Ogdoad consisted of four divine couples, each representing fundamental aspects of existence. These pairs of gods and goddesses were:

- **Nun and Naunet**: This couple represented the primordial waters (sacred waters that were bel, symbolizing the boundless expanse of the universe.

- **Heh and Hauhet**: These gods represented infinity and eternity. They embodied the endlessness of time and space.
- **Kek and Kauket**: These two represented darkness and obscurity, as well as the mysterious depths of the cosmos.
- **Amun and Amaunet:** Finally, these gods represented hiddenness and concealment, and they hid the secrets of creation from mortal eyes.

Together, these eight deities formed the foundation upon which the world was built, each contributing their divine essence to shape the universe.

The Role of the Ogdoad

As the first generation of deities, the Ogdoad played a crucial role in the creation and maintenance of cosmic order. They were also revered as the guardians of Ma'at (truth, balance, and harmony). Their power helped keep the forces of chaos in check, allowing life to flourish and thrive.

The Legacy of the Ogdoad

Though the Ogdoad faded into obscurity as Egypt's religious beliefs evolved over time, their legacy endured in the hearts and minds of the people. They were honored in temple rituals and revered as the ancestors of all the subsequent gods and goddesses. Even as newer deities gained importance, the Ogdoad remained a symbol of the ancient and eternal forces that govern the cosmos.

And so, dear adventurers, we conclude our tale of the Ogdoad. As we journey through the sands of time, let us remember the ancient wisdom of these divine beings and the profound impact they had on the creation and the world around them.

The Story of Sinuhe: Exile and Return

Lets move from the gods back into the mortal world to embark on a journey with an Egyptian official named Sinuhe. Sinuhe experienced a life full of adventure, danger, and eventually, a heartwarming return to his homeland. So, fasten your seatbelts, as we travel back in time to accompany Sinuhe on his adventures.

Who Was Sinuhe?

Sinuhe was a nobleman who served at the Egyptian court during the reign of Pharaoh Amenemhat I. He was a trusted and loyal servant, living a life of comfort and respect within the palace walls. But

Sinuhe's life soon took a dramatic turn that led him on a journey across foreign lands.

One day, while on a military campaign, Sinuhe received shocking news: Pharaoh Amenemhat I had been assassinated. Fearing that he too might be in danger, Sinuhe panicked and fled Egypt. With a heavy heart, he left behind everything he knew and loved. His quick departure was not out of disloyalty to his king, but out of fear for his own life.

Sinuhe's Life in Exile

Sinuhe's escape led him to the land of Canaan, where he sought refuge among strangers. Despite his fears and the uncertainty of living in exile, Sinuhe adapted to his new life. He married a local woman and was welcomed by the chief of a tribe, who admired Sinuhe's Egyptian wisdom and skills. Sinuhe even fought battles alongside his new companions, earning respect and wealth in his adopted land.

A Warrior in a Foreign Land

As years passed, Sinuhe became a celebrated warrior and a man of status among his new community. He was given land and servants, and he built a life that many would envy. However, despite his success and the peace he had found, Sinuhe's heart remained in Egypt. He missed his home and dreamed of returning to serve under the new pharaoh.

The Pharaoh's Invitation

One day, a message arrived from Egypt. The new Pharaoh, Senusret I, had heard of Sinuhe's plight and invited him to return to Egypt. The pharaoh offered Sinuhe forgiveness and promised him a place of honor back home. Overwhelmed with emotion, Sinuhe prepared to leave his life in Canaan behind to return to the land of his birth.

The Return to Egypt

Sinuhe's return to Egypt was triumphant and emotional. He was received with honors and given estates (a lot of land and servants) by the pharaoh. The people celebrated his return. Now back in his homeland, Sinuhe was overwhelmed with joy. He visited the tomb of his old king, Amenemhat I, and paid his respects, feeling that he had completed the circle of his life.

Sinuhe's Reflections

In his old age, Sinuhe wrote down his story, reflecting on his adventures and the lessons he had learned. He spoke of the value of humility, the importance of home, and the kindness of strangers. Sinuhe's story became a legendary tale in Egypt, told and retold as a testament to the strength of the human spirit in the face of adversity.

Today, Sinuhe's story teaches us that though life can take unexpected turns, courage and adaptability can help us overcome challenges. It also reminds us of the power of forgiveness and the importance of treasuring where we come from.

Unearthing the Past: Archaeological Discoveries and Their Global Fascination

In reality, these myths from ancient times have been brought back to life through the fascinating work of archaeologists. Today, let's put on our explorer hats and delve into the world of archaeology, where every discovery helps to piece together the vast, intricate puzzle of human history. In this section, we're going to explore how modern adventurers unearth secrets that have been buried for millennia. From magnificent tombs to the mysterious Rosetta Stone, each discovery has helped us connect with a past that, though ancient, feels closer with every brushstroke. So, let's start digging!

What is Archaeology?

Archaeology is the study of old things left behind by people from the past, such as bones, pots, tools, buildings, or even entire cities buried under the ground! Archaeologists are like detectives, but instead of solving crimes, they solve mysteries about how people lived long ago.

Discovering Ancient Egypt

Egypt is a treasure trove for archaeologists because it was one of the most advanced civilizations of its time. The dry desert climate of Egypt helped preserve many of these treasures in amazing condition, giving us clear snapshots of the past.

So, why do people find Egyptian archaeology so fascinating? Well, it's like putting together a giant puzzle of human history. Each discovery tells us more about how people lived, what they believed, and what they valued. Egypt's pyramids, mummies, and golden treasures tell tales of a world that seems almost magical.

These discoveries don't just help us learn; they also bring people together. Museums around the world display Egyptian artifacts, allowing everyone to share in their wonder. When archaeologists uncover something new, it can be headline news around the globe, sparking the imaginations of kids and adults alike.

Even today, new discoveries in Egypt are being made all the time. Just recently, archaeologists found new tombs, statues, and even entire workshops where ancient Egyptians made artifacts for the afterlife. Each new find helps fill in the blanks of history and teaches us more about this fascinating culture.

It is important to protect these exciting discoveries. Archaeologists work hard to make sure that ancient artifacts can be studied without damage. They are like guardians of history, making sure that future generations can also learn and be amazed by these treasures. Remember, the past is like a book waiting to be read, and archaeology is how we turn the pages.

The Rosetta Stone and the Decoding of Hieroglyphs

One of the most remarkable pages ever turned in the history of archaeology involves the Rosetta Stone, an artifact that unlocked the long-lost language of the ancient Egyptians. Imagine finding a huge puzzle piece that helps solve a puzzle that's been mixed up for thousands of years. That's what the Rosetta Stone is! It's a big slab of black rock called granodiorite, and it was found by French soldiers in Egypt in 1799 near a town called Rosetta (Rashid). What makes this stone super special is that it has the same message written in three different scripts: Greek, Demotic, and Ancient Egyptian Hieroglyphs (their written language).

Why Was the Rosetta Stone Important?

For many years, nobody knew how to read ancient Egyptian hieroglyphs. They were a complete mystery! People could see beautiful symbols on tomb walls and artifacts, but didn't know how to read them. When the Rosetta Stone was discovered, it was like finding a secret key because one of the languages written on it—Greek—was already well-known. This meant that if you could read Greek, you could figure out what the Egyptian hieroglyphs were saying too!

The Challenge of Decoding

Decoding the hieroglyphs wasn't easy. It was trickier than trying to solve the hardest crossword puzzle in the world because the hieroglyphs were pictures that could represent either sounds or whole ideas. Many smart scholars tried to decode them, but the real hero of our story is a man named Jean-François Champollion.

Jean-François Champollion Cracks the Code

Champollion was a French scholar who loved languages. He was fascinated by the Rosetta Stone and worked very hard to understand the hieroglyphs. In 1822, after years of studying, Champollion finally figured it out! He realized that some of the hieroglyphs represented the sounds of the Egyptian language, much like letters in the alphabet. This breakthrough was huge—it meant that at last, people could read the ancient words written thousands of years ago by the Egyptians.

Champollion used the Greek text on the Rosetta Stone as a guide. He knew that all the texts would say the same thing, so he compared them. By looking at names of rulers like Ptolemy and Cleopatra, which appeared in both the Greek and hieroglyph sections, he started to match sounds to symbols. Slowly but surely, he unlocked the language of the ancient Egyptians.

The Impact of Decoding Hieroglyphs

Once Champollion cracked the code, a whole new world opened up. Scholars could finally read the texts on temple walls, in tombs, and on ancient scrolls. They learned about Egyptian history, religion, and everyday life in incredible detail. It was like listening to the voices of people who had lived thousands of years ago.

Today, the Rosetta Stone is one of the most famous artifacts in the world, and it now lives in the British Museum in London. People from all over the world come to see it because it represents a great human achievement: the power of curiosity and intelligence to unlock the secrets of the past.

So, thanks to this incredible discovery and the genius of Champollion, we can now understand the messages left behind by the ancient Egyptians. The story of the Rosetta Stone shows us that with persistence and clever thinking, no mystery is too great to solve.

Egyptian Mythology in Modern Media

Thanks to the Rosetta Stone and Champollion's discovery, the exciting Egyptian tales from long ago haven't stayed in the past; instead, they've traveled all the way into today's movies, books, and video games! In this section we're going to see how ancient Egyptian myths have influenced some of your favorite stories and games. Let's jump on a magical carpet ride and discover how these old legends are still sparking fun and adventure in our modern world!

Egyptian Mythology in Movies

One of the most exciting ways Egyptian mythology comes to life is through movies. Filmmakers have long been fascinated by the rich stories and colorful characters of ancient Egypt. Have you ever seen a movie where a mummy comes to life? Many of these films are inspired by tales of curses and magic from Egyptian myths.

For example, the movie series "The Mummy" showcases adventures that blend real myths with fictional stories. These movies often feature exciting explorations of pyramids and encounters with creatures from Egyptian lore, like the fearsome god Anubis and various mummies. While these films take a lot of creative liberties, they also encourage audiences to learn more about the actual stories behind the characters.

Egyptian Gods in Books

Many authors have been inspired to write books that bring Egyptian mythology into the lives of their characters. Rick Riordan, for example, wrote a series called The Kane Chronicles, where modern-day kids discover they are connected to powerful Egyptian gods like Horus and Set. These books mix action-packed adventures with fun facts about ancient Egypt, making learning about mythology exciting and relatable.

Books like these help young readers imagine what it would be like to interact with the gods and goddesses of Egypt. They also explore themes of bravery, family, and destiny, which are all common elements in ancient myths.

Video Games and Egyptian Mythology

Video games also offer a dynamic way to experience the world of Egyptian mythology. One popular game, "Assassin's Creed: Origins," takes players on a journey through a digital recreation of ancient Egypt, where they can explore detailed environments that look like the real historical sites. Players meet characters from Egyptian history and mythology and engage in quests that involve famous myths and legends.

These games are not just about having fun; they're also about stepping into the shoes of someone from ancient times and experiencing their world. This helps players learn history in an immersive way.

Why Is Egyptian Mythology So Popular in the Media?

One reason Egyptian mythology is so popular in modern media is because of how vibrant and visual these myths are. The stories are full of dramatic conflicts, heroic deeds, and mystical creatures, which make them perfect for creative adaptations. The gods and goddesses, with their animal heads and fantastic powers, capture our imaginations and offer endless possibilities for storytelling.

Learning from Myths in Modern Media

While enjoying these modern adaptations, it's good to remember that they are often not entirely accurate to the historical myths. They are meant to entertain and inspire, leading to a deeper interest in learning about the real stories and history of ancient Egypt. This is why it's fun and useful to read books, visit museums, or even watch documentaries about ancient Egypt alongside enjoying its mythology in movies and games.

Chapter Conclusion

As our journey through the myths of ancient Egypt draws to a close, let us pause to reflect on the wonders we have encountered and lessons we have learned. From the epic tales of creation to the heroic exploits of gods and mortals, these stories have captivated our imaginations and illuminated the mysteries of a bygone era.

Through exploring the myths of ancient Egypt, we have uncovered timeless truths about the human experience, such as love and loss, courage and sacrifice, and the enduring quest for meaning. Through the lens of mythology, we have glimpsed the rich tapestry of human existence, woven with threads of hope, resilience, and the boundless potential of the human spirit.

But our journey does not end here. The legacy of ancient Egypt lives on, not only in the stories we have encountered but also in the archaeological wonders that continue to inspire awe and wonder. From the towering pyramids to the enigmatic hieroglyphs, each artifact is a testament to the ingenuity and creativity of a civilization that flourished millennia ago.

As we bid farewell to the myths of ancient Egypt, let us carry with us the wisdom and wonder they impart. Let us remember the lessons of the gods and goddesses, the triumphs of heroes, and the enduring power of storytelling to illuminate the human condition. And let us be inspired to seek out our own adventures, to uncover the mysteries that lie hidden in the sands of time, and to embrace the legacy of ancient Egypt as a beacon of hope and inspiration for generations to come.

CHAPTER 6: HEROES AND LEGENDS

Now that we've covered some of ancient Egypt's most interesting legends, get ready to meet some of the most amazing people from the past. These heroes did incredible things and became legends because of their bravery, smarts, and kindness. We'll explore exciting stories about an architect who designed a giant pyramid, a scribe who went on a wild adventure, and a wise advisor who shared important lessons with everyone. Each story is full of surprises and big dreams!

So, grab your explorer's hat and let's set off on an adventure to discover the incredible lives of these legendary figures. Are you ready to find out what makes someone a hero? Let's go!

Imhotep: The Architect Who Became a God

Long ago, in the dusty sands of ancient Egypt, lived Imhotep, whose name means "he who comes in peace." He did not start out as a pharaoh or a prince, but rather was born as a commoner in the city of Memphis. Despite his status as a commoner,

Imhotep was incredibly smart and talented. He served under the Pharaoh Djoser as an architect, priest, engineer, and physician.

The Architect of the First Pyramid

Imhotep's most famous achievement was designing the Step Pyramid at Saqqara. This pyramid was the very first of its kind—it was a structure so magnificent and unique that it set the standard for all future pyramids. The Step Pyramid was originally built as a simple tomb for Pharaoh Djoser, but Imhotep had a grand vision. He expanded it into a towering six-layered structure that stretched up to the heavens, unlike anything ever seen before.

Imhotep the Physician

Imhotep was also a pioneering physician that wrote medical texts. His writings were used for centuries after his death to help with treatment of diseases and injuries. The texts described treatments with such skill that people believed Imhotep was blessed by the gods. In fact, Imhotep's approach to medicine was so advanced that he is often called the "Father of Medicine," long before Hippocrates ever was!

A Man of Wisdom and Knowledge

Imhotep was also known for his wisdom and deep knowledge of the arts, science, and literature. He served as the high priest of the sun god Ra, which was a position of great honor. His wise sayings and proverbs were famous among the Egyptians, and his advice was sought by many. He was a true polymath, which means he knew a lot about many different subjects!

Imhotep's Legacy

Because of his brilliant contributions to Egyptian society, Imhotep was deified, which means he was turned into a god after his death. This was a rare honor usually reserved only for pharaohs. As a god, Imhotep was worshiped as the patron of scribes and the healer of the sick. People prayed to him for wisdom, health, and guidance. Many temples were also built in his honor.

Today, thousands of years later, Imhotep's legacy still shines bright. He is remembered not only as a great architect and physician but also as a symbol of human potential. His journey from a common man to a god demonstrates that with talent, hard work, and kindness, anyone can achieve greatness.

Ptah-hotep: The Wise Vizier and His Maxims

Now, let's move on to meet Ptah-hotep, an ancient Egyptian vizier who was famous for his wisdom. His teachings have been passed down through the ages, and today we'll discover why his words still matter. Get ready to learn from a master of ancient wisdom!

Ptah-hotep served as a vizier—the highest official to serve the king—under the Pharaoh Djedkare Isesi during Egypt's Fifth Dynasty, around 2400 BCE. This was a time when Egypt was flourishing, so wise counsel was highly valued. Ptah-hotep was not only a political advisor but also a revered sage (very intelligent person) whose ideas on ethics and proper conduct were written down in a collection known as "The Maxims of Ptah-hotep."

The Maxims of Ptah-hotep

The "Maxims of Ptah-hotep" is one of the oldest books in the world. Here, Ptah-hotep wrote down advice on how to live a good life, based on principles of justice, kindness, and respect for others. His maxims teach us how to handle conflicts, be good leaders, and find harmony in our lives.

Here are a few of his wise sayings:

- "Be a good listener—it is a source of strength."
- "If you are a leader, listen calmly to the speech of one who pleads."
- "Do not be proud of your knowledge, consult the ignorant and the wise."

Ptah-hotep's Role as Vizier

As vizier, Ptah-hotep's job was to ensure that the kingdom ran smoothly. This meant overseeing the administration, legal matters, and the treasury. His role required wisdom, fairness, and a deep understanding of people. So, his maxims were not just philosophical thoughts but practical advice for dealing with daily responsibilities in ways that promoted peace and fairness.

Teaching Through Stories

Ptah-hotep often used simple stories and parables to illustrate his points. This made his lessons easy to understand and remember, even for young people. He believed that wisdom came from listening carefully and thinking deeply, which were both qualities that he tried to instill in others through his teachings.

Why Ptah-hotep Matters Today

Ptah-hotep's teachings are still relevant because they speak to universal truths about human behavior and social justice. His call for humility, thoughtful listening, and respectful communication are qualities that help us build better relationships and stronger communities even today.

The story of Ptah-hotep, the Wise Vizier, teaches us that true wisdom comes from understanding and respecting one another. His life and maxims show us that the keys to a harmonious society are kindness, fairness, and education. As we close this chapter, remember that the ancient lessons of Ptah-hotep can still guide us in our daily lives.

The Legend of Moses

Now, let's embark on an epic journey through the sands of time to uncover the incredible story of Moses—the courageous religious leader who changed the course of history!

Our tale begins in the Land of Goshen, a land blessed by the Nile's fertile waters and home to the Israelites, who were the chosen people of the Christian god according to legend. It was here that Moses was born, a child destined for greatness in a time of hardship. Though he was born into a world where slavery was rampant and cruelty reigned supreme, Moses would rise to become a beacon of hope for his people.

A Leader Emerges

As Moses grew, he witnessed firsthand the injustices suffered by his fellow Israelites at the hands of their Egyptian masters. Slavery was a common practice in ancient Egypt. As such, the Israelites were stripped of their humanity by their oppressors. But Moses refused to stand idly by while his people suffered. He knew that he was destined for something greater and had a divine purpose to fulfill.

The Exodus

Driven by a deep sense of justice and guided by the hand of destiny, Moses embarked on a courageous quest to free his people from bondage. With unwavering faith and unyielding determination, he led the Israelites on a daring journey out of Egypt and into the wilderness beyond. Though it was dangerous and difficult, Moses never gave up.

The Lawgiver

As they journeyed through the desert, Moses received divine guidance from the "Almighty" (his Christian god). He climbed Mount Sinai, where he received the Ten Commandments—divine laws that his god had created to serve as the foundation of a just and righteous society. So, Moses became not only a liberator but also a lawgiver, bestowing upon his people the gift of freedom and the wisdom to govern themselves with justice and compassion.

Legacy and Inspiration

Though Moses's time on Earth has long since passed, his legacy endures as a symbol of courage, compassion, and unwavering faith. His story has inspired countless generations to stand up against oppression, fight for justice, and never lose hope in the face of adversity. From the banks of the Nile to the shores of distant lands, the tale of Moses continues to captivate the hearts and minds of people around the world.

The Remarkable Life of Ibn Khaldun

After discussing one of Christianity's most famous icons, we now move on to a lesser-known legend named Ibn Khaldun. Ibn Khaldun was born into a wealthy and influential family. Despite his privileged upbringing, Ibn Khaldun faced many challenges during his youth. Tragedy struck when he lost his parents at a young age, which thrust him into a world of hardship and uncertainty. But even in the face of these difficulties, Ibn Khaldun was still hungry for knowledge.

Ibn Khaldun was blessed with a keen intellect and a passion for learning. He studied under the guidance of respected teachers and scholars, soaking up knowledge like a sponge. But Ibn Khaldun's quest for wisdom extended beyond the confines of the classroom—he was a tireless reader and seeker of truth. Despite his wealth, Ibn Khaldun faced many obstacles on his path to enlightenment. However, his determination could not be stopped.

A Voice of Dissent

As Ibn Khaldun matured, he became increasingly disappointed with the complexities of politics and governance. He witnessed firsthand the corruption and injustice that were like a sickness in his society. So, he decided to speak out against tyranny and oppression. But his outspoken views came at a cost—when he dared to challenge the status quo, he was put in prison. Yet even in the darkest of times, Ibn Khaldun remained true to his beliefs.

Scholar and Philosopher

Upon his release from prison, Ibn Khaldun embarked on a new chapter of his life as a scholar and philosopher. He poured his insights and observations into writing, publishing numerous books that would shape the course of intellectual history. His magnum opus, "The Muqaddimah," is a masterpiece of historical analysis and social theory. It even laid the groundwork for modern sociology and historiography, which are two very important fields of study about humans and history.

Legacy and Impact

Ibn Khaldun's writings transcended the boundaries of time and space, resonating with readers across generations and continents. His profound insights into society, culture, and human behavior continue to inspire scholars and thinkers to this day. Ibn Khaldun's legacy endures as a testament to the power of knowledge and resilience. May his story serve as a beacon of inspiration for all who dare to dream, question, and seek the truth in an uncertain world.

Muhammad Ali: The Father of Modern Egypt

Now let's move on from one of Egypt's greatest thinkers to one of its greatest leaders! , We'll now delve into the remarkable story of Muhammad Ali—the visionary leader known as the "Father of Modern Egypt." Join us as we uncover his journey of reform and transformation as he forever changed the course of Egyptian history!

Muhammad Ali was a trailblazer, reformist, and visionary leader who left an important mark on the sands of time. As he was born in the late 18th century, Muhammad Ali rose to prominence during a period of great change and conflict in Egypt.

A Man of Vision

From an early age, Muhammad Ali possessed a bold and modern vision for Egypt's future. He recognized the need to modernize Egypt's military and institutions, laying the groundwork for a stronger, more prosperous nation.

Modernization and Reform

Muhammad Ali wasted no time in reforming Egypt. He rapidly modernized the military, cultivating a skilled Egyptian elite trained in European academic institutions. Under his leadership, Egypt underwent a period of unprecedented transformation, embracing new technologies, industries, and ideas.

Legacy of Leadership

Muhammad Ali's legacy as the "Father of Modern Egypt" is celebrated by Egyptians far and wide. His tireless efforts to elevate Egypt's status on the world stage earned him the respect and admiration for centuries to come.

And so, dear readers, we bid farewell to Muhammad Ali—the visionary leader whose legacy continues to inspire and uplift the people of Egypt. May his story serve as enduring inspiration and remind us of the power of leadership, vision, and determination.

Chapter Conclusion

From Muhammad Ali's role in profound change to Imhotep's many talents, these stories show us that anyone can achieve greatness. Whether it's through building magnificent structures, embarking on daring adventures, or sharing wise words to guide others, each hero we met had their own unique way of leaving a mark on the world. These men and legends prove that bravery, intelligence, and kindness never go out of style.

Remember, heroes aren't just characters in stories; they're real people who do extraordinary things. Maybe one day, you'll tell your own heroic tale! Keep dreaming big, staying curious, and learning from those who came before us. Who knows? Maybe you're the next great hero in the making!

CONCLUSION

As our journey through the land of ancient Egypt draws to a close, we bid farewell to the legendary figures, majestic monuments, and timeless tales that have captivated our hearts and minds. From the towering pyramids of Giza to the mystical rituals of mummification, we have explored the many wonders of a civilization that has left a lasting mark on history.

As we reflect on the stories we have encountered, we are reminded of the rich tapestry of culture, tradition, and mythology that defined ancient Egypt. We have witnessed the power and majesty of the pharaohs, the wisdom and strength of the queens, and the divine grace of the gods and goddesses who ruled over the heavens and the earth.

Through the tales of heroes and legends, we have learned valuable lessons of courage, resilience, and compassion. From the visionary leaders who transformed their kingdom to the ordinary people who dared to defy the odds, each story has inspired us to dream big, overcome obstacles, and strive for greatness.

So, though our journey may be coming to an end, the spirit of ancient Egypt lives on in our hearts and minds. As we close the pages of this book, we carry with us the memories of the pharaohs, the echoes of the gods, and the timeless wisdom of the ages. Let us cherish these stories and pass them on to future generations, so that the legacy of ancient Egypt may endure for all time.

And so, dear readers, we bid farewell to the cradle of civilization. May the magic of ancient Egypt continue to inspire and enchant us, guiding us on new adventures and discoveries.

Until we meet again, may the sands of time carry your dreams to distant shores, where the legacy of Egypt shines bright as the stars in the night sky.

Bye for now!

THE EXTRA PART

So now that we've journeyed through the magnificent stories of ancient Egypt, met powerful pharaohs, glamorous queens, and learned about mighty gods and legendary heroes,, let's check how much you've remembered. Take this quiz to see how many correct answers you can get. Are you ready to prove that you're a true historian of ancient Egypt?

Why is King Tutankhamun often referred to as "The Boy King"?

A) He became pharaoh at a very old age.
B) He was known for his youthful energy.
C) He became pharaoh when he was very young.
D) He ruled for a very long time.

What is Pharaoh Djoser best known for?

A) Building the first true pyramid.
B) His military conquests.
C) Establishing the first schools in Egypt.
D) Writing important laws.

What title is Ramses II often given due to his achievements?

A) The Great Architect.
B) The Great and Powerful.
C) The Great Explorer.
D) The Great Writer.

What major change did Akhenaten bring during his reign?

A) He introduced the worship of many gods.
B) He banned the worship of all gods but one, Aten.
C) He improved the economy.
D) He wrote a famous book.

What was Snefru known for in ancient Egypt?

A) Building a famous temple.
B) Constructing several pyramids.
C) His long peaceful reign.
D) Discovering papyrus.

How did Queen Hatshepsut make her mark as a ruler of Egypt?

A) She was known for her beautiful singing.
B) She dressed as a man to assert her authority as pharaoh.
C) She wrote a popular book on governance.
D) She discovered gold mines.

What was the primary purpose of mummification?

A) To ensure the deceased looked their best.
B) To protect the dead from wildlife.
C) To preserve the body for the afterlife.
D) To mark the social status of the deceased.

Ra was the god of…?

A) The underworld.
B) The moon.
C) The sun.
D) The ocean.

In The Tale of the Shipwrecked Sailor, what unusual character does the sailor meet?

A) A talking hippopotamus.
B) A giant serpent king.
C) A ghost of a pharaoh.
D) An enchanted cat.

What is Ptah-hotep best remembered for?

A) His military strategies.
B) His architectural designs.
C) His maxims or wise sayings.
D) His treasure discoveries.

ANSWERS

C) He became pharaoh when he was very young.

A) Building the first true pyramid.

B) The Great and Powerful.

B) He banned the worship of all gods but one, Aten.

B) Constructing several pyramids.

B) She dressed as a man to assert her authority as pharaoh.

C) To preserve the body for the afterlife.

C) The sun.

B) A giant serpent king.

C) His maxims or wise sayings.

THE EXTRA, EXTRA PART

These riddles are designed to test your knowledge about the fascinating world of ancient Egypt. Each one relates to the pharaohs, queens, gods, and mythical tales we've discussed. So, put on your thinking caps! Are you prepared to decode these enigmas and discover hidden truths? Grab a pencil, gather your friends, and see who can solve these ancient puzzles first!

Pharaohs and Pyramids:

I was made of stone and stood for eternity, a tomb for Pharaoh but without a key. What am I?

Mystical Queens:

I ruled as a king but was not a man, under my reign Egypt expanded its span. Who am I?

Gods and Goddesses:

I have the head of a falcon, and the sun is my mark, I protect the Pharaohs even in the dark. Who am I?

Legendary Creatures:

Part man and part lion, I guard and protect, solving my riddle you must not neglect. What am I?

The Afterlife:

I am not alive, but I walk and talk, preserved for eternity, in bandages I'm locked. What am I?

Hieroglyphics:

Symbols and pictures that speak without sound, and in tombs and temples, with me, messages are found. What am I?

Ancient Wisdom:

I am old but wise, with advice in a book, to find a life of harmony, in my pages, you should look. Who am I?

Heroic Tales:

I left my home under a cloud of fear, but returned a hero, to the land I hold dear. Who am I?

ANSWERS

Pharaohs and Pyramids:
Answer: A pyramid.

Mystical Queens:
Answer: Queen Hatshepsut.

Gods and Goddesses:
Answer: Horus.

Legendary Creatures:
Answer: The Sphinx.

The Afterlife:
Answer: A mummy.

Hieroglyphics:
Answer: Hieroglyphics.

Ancient Wisdom:
Answer: Ptah-hotep.

Heroic Tales:
Answer: Sinuhe.

Made in United States
North Haven, CT
03 December 2024